Teaching and Learning in Communities of Faith

Linda J. Vogel

TEACHING AND LEARNING
IN
COMMUNITIES OF FAITH

Empowering Adults
Through
Religious Education

Jossey-Bass Publishers • San Francisco

Substantial discounts on bulk quantities of Jossey-Bass books are available to corporations, professional associations, and other organizations. For details and discount information, contact the special sales department at Jossey-Bass Inc., Publishers (415) 433-1740; Fax (800) 605-2665.

Jossey-Bass Web address: http://www.josseybass.com

 Manufactured in the United States of America on Lyons Falls Turin Book. This paper is acid-free and 100 percent totally chlorine-free.

Credits are on p. 219.

Library of Congress Cataloging-in-Publication Data

Vogel, Linda J.
    Teaching and learning in communities of faith : empowering adults
through religious education / Linda J. Vogel.—1st ed.
        p.   cm.—(The Jossey-Bass higher and adult education series)
    Includes bibliographical references and index.
    ISBN 1-55542-390-6 (alk. paper)
    1. Religious education of adults. I. Title. II. Series.
    BL42.V64   1991
    268'.434—dc20   91-21686

HB Printing   10 9 8 7 6 5 4 3 2

PB Printing   10 9 8 7 6 5 4 3 2 1

The Jossey-Bass
Higher and Adult Education Series

Consulting Editor
Adult and Continuing Education

Alan B. Knox
University of Wisconsin, Madison

Dedicated to the memory of
JENNIFER PURDY,
whose eighteen years
exemplified
the joy of learning in a world
where no one has to be an outsider

CONTENTS

PREFACE

The task of adult religious education is to create settings and processes that invite people to journey together—exploring, reflecting, experiencing, and acting in and toward faith. Religious education is about hearing and sharing stories; about talking together, listening, and making connections; about promise, obedience, pathos, and mystery; about sharing hope for the future and seeking peace. Adult religious education invites teachers and learners to journey together toward knowing, loving, and serving the living God. It is a journey toward wholeness.

Disruptions in our lives require us to discover new ways of thinking and acting. Adults struggle with issues relating to family life, work, school, church or synagogue, and uses of leisure time. Adults experience confusion and anxiety over their personal future and that of the whole creation. Health care needs, education for themselves and their children, environmental and economic issues that often seem to be in conflict, and the meaning and costs of peace and war disrupt and challenge the ways people learn and act.

Adult religious education can provide a hospitable space where people feel at home enough to struggle with hard questions and to risk looking at alternative answers. Adult religious education is grounded in a faith story. For Jews it is the story of Abraham and Sarah, Moses, David, the prophets, and the Talmud; for Christians the story includes Jesus, Mary Magdalene, Peter, Paul, Lydia, and the church through the ages. As adults engage in religious education, the stories and rituals, beliefs, and life-styles of their faith community intersect and foster dialogue with the experiences and dilemmas adults face in today's world.

As we share our experiences with others and listen to their stories, we are empowered to reflect and discern, to decide and act. Making connections with our own past and present and our future hopes; others' experiences and hopes; and the stories, beliefs, rituals, and values of our faith community helps us make and discover meaning and nourishes our souls. Adult religious education that is dynamic, flexible, and creative can help people grow toward knowing what they see instead of being bound by continuing to see what they know.

Sharing stories and claiming a faith story as our own lead to authentic celebration. Persons who are journeying in and toward faith are called both to celebrate and to care. Adult religious education involves human beings in communities of faith in seeking to know and imagine, to integrate and act, as they reframe questions and risk seeing and hearing in new ways; these can inspire care and love as people make connections with past, present, and future and grow in their relationships with self, others, the whole creation, and God.

Teaching and learning in communities of faith must incorporate a dialogue—where all have an opportunity both to listen and to be heard. Teaching begins with what people already know and offers tools for working toward a consensus where all can benefit. In this book we will assess tools that help people examine and give a name to their assumptions; we will consider ways of offering support, challenge, and vision. Setting forth questions and introducing methods that invite critical reflection and creative imagination can encourage human beings to begin caring and risking as they journey toward a love-filled, justice-seeking world.

Adult religious education is the lifelong process of intentional engagement with the faith story of our particular faith community, with our own stories, and with those of all people and communities. These compel us to listen to others, to build community, to clarify problems, and then to work toward a more just world. Those who choose to journey with me through this book will explore the world where we live (which is the context for all religious teaching and learning), the ways adults learn and grow, and metaphors for understanding how individuals and faith communities approach adult religious education. We will explore one model for engaging in teaching and learning with adults in communities of faith. The reader is invited to enter into the dialogue, to discover new questions, and to continue journeying in faith—sorting out what will be useful and leaving the rest behind. It is an invitation to celebrate and care, to grow and serve. It is an invitation to learn—in community—to love God more deeply and to serve God more faithfully.

Part One examines needs that adult religious education is called to consider. It provides the context and sets the stage for exploring the ways people of faith journey through life. Using metaphor and story, this section investigates how adults can be helped to make sense of their world and to find nourishment for their souls as they move toward faith. Chapter One focuses on why and how we need to learn the language of our faith community, as well as the languages of others in our world, so that we can grow in our own faith and enter into dialogue with those of other religious communities. It attends to our ways of knowing as we seek to grow in faith. Chapter Two invites us to take seriously and examine the larger context in which we live and learn. It explores the importance of the ways we think and speak about life and death as we seek to live faithfully in relationship to God and to others.

Part Two focuses on a variety of ways of understanding and engaging in adult religious education. Chapter Three explores how adults learn as they move through the life span. Chapter Four offers four metaphors—schooling, faith community, pilgrimage, and the new earth—that suggest differing approaches to adult religious education. These four metaphors provide pieces of a puzzle that may help people of differing faith traditions as they seek to create the paths for their individual and collective journeys. Chapters Five and Six offer a model for fostering teaching and learning in Christian communities that grows out of an examination of the gospel accounts of Jesus feeding the five thousand. As we shall see in these chapters, Jesus gives us an example for teaching and learning:

People of faith are
called to be

in touch with the world
as well as
in touch with God.
By
creating a hospitable space,
people discover that
God's Word touches the world.
By being open to
glimpses of God's perspective
that are celebrated in the
breaking of bread,
people begin
sharing with disciples who, in turn, share
in ways that offer
more than enough for all.
People of faith are asked to
gather the leftovers
as they participate in God's all-inclusive, justice-seeking
reign and realm that both is and is coming to be.

Part Three focuses on paths that adult religious education offers to groups of learners struggling to discern meaning in life and death in ways that lead to wholeness and a more just and harmonious world. Chapter Seven examines underlying assumptions and strategies for building foundations to nourish souls as people come to know and claim their community's faith story and grow toward more faithful living in light of their own stories, traditions, rituals, values, and life-styles. A foundation that holds possibilities for Christian religious education is offered. Religious educators of other faith communities who are committed to an openness to truth and who seek a more just and humane world may find insights and tools that can prove helpful as they examine and build their own foundations. Chapter Eight focuses on ways of developing programs for adult religious education in communities of faith as they seek to embody their own models. Chapter Nine explores ways of teaching and learning and suggests methods that may be useful for those who teach adults in communities of faith. Chapter Ten is concerned with making connections, sharing power, and reaching out to those outside our own faith community in order to begin listening, talking, and working with all who share our vision for justice and peace. It highlights courses of action and strategies for those who seek to journey through adulthood in and toward faith.

Whoever seeks to write a book on religious education faces the dilemma of balancing the desire to explore broad, all-inclusive questions of journeying in (any) faith against the need to own one's identity as a person of a particular faith. I am a Christian, a fact all those who accompany me through these pages should know. But I am also a person who recognizes that there are many paths to faith and that my path is not the only, or even the only Christian, path. I desire to learn from others even as I hope my experience may be useful to those whose faith journeys are different from mine. I have tried to draw on some other faith traditions and to provide an opportunity for those in other traditions to appropriate certain underlying principles and assumptions by filling them with their own faith-story content. It is my deep hope and my prayer that this book on adult religious education—written from the perspective I know best—will add to the dialogue about making and discovering meaning and about nourishing souls.

I invite you to explore with me what it means to know that "we are still God's people; the journey is our home" (see Ruth Duck's hymn "Lead On, O Cloud of Presence," in Hawkes and Hamill, 1984, p. 192).

Acknowledgments

All who have taught and learned with me throughout my adult life have contributed—both knowingly and unknowingly, through good experiences and bad—to the growing understanding that has taken shape in this book. The teacher-learner with whom I have chosen to share my adult life—my husband and soul mate, Dwight Vogel—has contributed more than he can ever know. I am grateful for his love and care for me.

Colleagues, students, and friends have listened as I have sought to formulate my hunches, insights, and research into a unified whole. The congregation of St. Luke's United Methodist Church in Dubuque, Iowa, taught me as I taught and learned with them. Much of what we did together is reflected in this book. For taking time to read my manuscript and offer helpful comments, I am grateful to my covenant group at Garrett-Evangelical Theological Seminary—Joan Albrecht, Jon and Barbara Buxton, Glen Robinson, Ronald Rosinsky, and Carolin Sprague; to my good friend Diane Olson; and to my colleague Jack Seymour, with whom I greatly enjoy teaching and learning on this seminary faculty. I am also grateful to the United Methodist Association of Professors of Christian Education (UMAPCE) professors who have accepted me and encouraged me to grow and develop since we began meeting in 1974.

My consulting editor, Alan Knox, has been most helpful— the speed with which he responded to my questions, the insights and the sense of collegiality he offered are gifts I treasure. Gale Erlandson and Susan Abel have been both gracious and helpful as we prepared this manuscript for publication. I am grateful, too, to Garrett-Evangelical Theological Seminary for granting my sabbatical to complete this manuscript and to Linda Koops for her secretarial support.

It is my prayer that those who teach and learn in communities of faith will find in this book ways to foster a more humane world, where paths toward peace with justice and away from war and oppression can be discovered and shared.

Evanston, Illinois   Linda J. Vogel
September 1991

THE AUTHOR

Linda J. Vogel gains energy from teaching and learning with people of all ages and from many differing cultures. She has taught children, young people, and adults in public schools, the church, nursing home settings, and college and now teaches Christian education as a professor at Garrett-Evangelical Theological Seminary—a graduate school of theology of the United Methodist Church in Evanston, Illinois.

She received her B.S. degree (1962) in elementary education from Boston University, her M.R.E. degree (1964) from Andover Newton Theological Seminary, a graduate specialization in gerontology (1977) from the University of Nebraska, Omaha, and her Ph. D. degree (1981) in adult education from the University of Iowa. Before joining the seminary faculty, she taught and served as director of continuing education at Westmar College (1965–1985) and served as diaconal minister of education at St. Luke's United Methodist Church in Dubuque, Iowa (1985–1987).

A recipient of the John Leonard Davies Award for contributions to the field of adult education (University of Iowa, 1982), Vogel continues to seek ways to join with many around the world to make this planet more healthful, just, and harmonious.

She has led conferences and workshops in cities across the United States and has written church-school curricula for children and adults for the United Methodist Church and the National Council of Churches. Her recent publications include articles in

The Journal of Aging and Judaism, Leader in the Church School Today, Quarterly Review, Daughters of Sarah, and *The Christian Ministry.* Her books include *Teaching Older Adults* (1989), *The Religious Education of Older Adults* (1984), and *Helping a Child Understand Death* (1975).

Teaching and Learning
in
Communities of Faith

PART ONE

The Growing Hunger for Adult Religious Education

Part One focuses on the growing desire of people to make sense of life and death in ways that lead to integrity and wholeness. Chapter One uses scriptural metaphors to discover the words (languages) that one must know in order to engage in adult religious education; it also addresses the need for a different language that allows us to speak and listen effectively in the larger world community. It explores ways of knowing that can lead to living faith. Chapter Two examines the contexts for religious education (the world in both macrocosm and microcosm) and explores the roles of theology in faithful learning and living. It examines metaphors and story as doors through which learners can engage in theologizing. It considers why it is crucial to *know* what we *see* rather than settling for *seeing* what we *know*.

ONE

How People of Faith
Journey Through Life

Every community that wants to last beyond a single generation must concern itself with education. Education has to
do with the maintenance of a community through the generations. This maintenance must assure enough continuity of
vision, value, and perception so that the community sus-
tains its self-identity. At the same time, such maintenance
must assure enough freedom and novelty so that the community can survive in and be pertinent to new circumstances. Thus, education must attend both to processes of
continuity and discontinuity in order to avoid fossilizing
into irrelevance on the one hand, and relativizing into disappearance on the other hand.
                                    —*Walter Brueggemann, 1982, p. 1*

Given the possibilities of "fossilizing into irrelevance" or "relativizing into disappearance," faith communities are called upon to
confront the challenge to become more purposeful about who and
whose they are so that they can find ways to share their story, vision,
values, and ways of being and doing with others. To be a viable
faith community necessitates our confronting as illusory the idea
that we can escape into our churches and synagogues; rather, as
faith communities we are called to embark on a journey. As Ruth
Duck's hymn, "Lead On, O Cloud of Presence," asserts, "We are

3

still God's people; the journey is our home" (Duck and Bausch, 1981).

In his spiritual autobiography, Robert McAfee Brown asserts that "our location is the journey itself. But we are always being dislocated, moving ourselves or being moved (sometimes kicking and screaming) to somewhere else along the journey. It is precisely dislocation that *makes* it a journey" (1980, p. 16).

The task of this book on adult religious education is to focus on how persons of faith within faith communities have journeyed toward that faithfulness and how adult religious education can offer vision and tools for our own journeys. Pain and joy, hope and despair, vocation and calling, are most often to be found in the journey itself. And just when one expects to arrive at one's destination, the road jogs or broadens, and one discovers that the journey has only just begun! It is a journey with God and toward God. It is the hope of our whole world.

Abraham and Sarah embarked in faith on a long journey to a far away and unknown place (Gen. 12–25:11). Their journey was not only to new surroundings and a new way of life; it was to a different way of understanding who they were and who God intended them to be; it was a journey that involved letting go of old ways of thinking and acting and of trusting untried ways of relating to God and others.

The Hebrew Bible is itself illustrative of a people's journeying with God. As Michael Fishbane declares, "The texts and traditions . . . of ancient Israel were not simply copied, studied, transmitted, or recited. They were . . . subject to redaction, elucidation, reformulation, and outright transformation. Accordingly, our received traditions are complex blends of *traditum* [the content of tradition] and *traditio* [the process of transmission] in dynamic interaction, dynamic interpenetration, and dynamic interdependence. They are, in sum, the exegetical voices of many teachers . . . , from different circles and times, responding to real and theoretical considerations as perceived and as anticipated" (1985, p. 543).

It is important that as religious educators we focus on the *living* Word of God. Paying attention to the canonical process of the Hebrew Bible can help us gain insight as we examine both the

Israelites' journey and the way the record of their journey evolved (see Brueggemann, 1982, pp. 6 ff.).

The first strand in the fabric of scripture is the Torah, which has come to be understood as the sum and substance of all that is included in the first five books of the Hebrew Bible (Genesis–Deuteronomy); a broader interpretation includes all of Jewish learnings (both written and oral). Its way of knowing is primarily narrative; as it evolved, it provided the early Hebrew community with stories of faith that offered a way of creating order out of chaos—a means of sculpting meaning.

The Torah is nonnegotiable; one does not argue or debate it. At the same time, the Torah does not claim to be all-knowing; it honors mystery. *Story* is its way of teaching—of socializing persons into the community. Brueggemann points out that "story as a distinctive way of epistemology is especially appropriate to the Torah and includes these points: (1) Story is concrete . . . , (2) Story is open-ended in its telling . . . , (3) Story in Israel was intended for the practice of imagination . . . , (4) Stories . . . are characteristically experiential . . . , and (5) Story is the bottom line" (1982, pp. 23-26). As Brueggemann states, Torah's mode of knowledge is authoritative and creates an ethos, a consensus, that engenders trust (1982, p. 91). *Promise* is its central claim (1982, p. 32). *Obedience* is the desired response (1982, pp. 102 ff.).

The second strand in the canonical process is the prophetic word. Although Torah is normative, the prophetic word is not; the prophets speak words that are "immediate, intrusive, and surprising" (Brueggemann, 1982, p. 41). Human beings must be a part of the consensus of the Torah in order to hear the questions and challenges spoken by the prophets. Here we find an alternative word. Without prophetic voices the consensus might wither and die. By challenging and disrupting it, the community's ethos is called continually to face the claims of a God who demands justice and who identifies with the poor and marginalized. The prophets introduce *pathos* and bring "new truth in uncredentialed channels" as they challenge the consensus with their "disruptive word" (Brueggemann, 1982, p. 91).

Finally, the Hebrew Bible includes writings and wisdom literature (for example, Song of Songs, Esther, Ruth, Lamentations,

Psalms, Proverbs, Job, Ecclesiastes) that reflect our struggles to discern and comprehend the meaning of freedom and responsibility, mystery and awe, living and dying. In these books, those who teach are more apt to question, speculate, and offer possible insights than they are to make assertions or claim authority. "Wisdom is the readiness both to penetrate the mystery and to live obediently with its inscrutability" (Brueggemann, 1982, p. 91).

These strands that make up the Hebrew Bible evolved over hundreds of years. Brueggemann characterizes them as "the disclosure of binding" (Torah), "the disruption for justice" (the prophetic voices), and "the discernment of order" (writings and wisdom). Certainly, the long prehistory and much of the history was shared around campfires and in homes long before it was put in written form. As it was passed from generation to generation, it was "detribalized and nationalized; depolytheized and monotheized, reorganized and reconceptualized" (Fishbane, 1985, p. 6). The Hebrew Bible, as well as the New Testament, reflects the journey of a people—its stories became their stories, and each generation claimed them for their own as they interpreted and (re)conceptualized them in light of their life experiences and the demands of the age and place in which they lived.

People of faith who live in a pluralistic world (as the Hebrews did and as we do) have to come to terms with how their own faith commitments are going to be carried out and shared with those who hold different commitments. Engaging in dialogue and honest sharing is one option; seeking to change those who are different is another; a third option is isolation and a refusal to communicate with any who do not speak one's own language or accept one's own presuppositions; or, finally, one can accommodate (adapt while retaining one's own identity) or assimilate (be absorbed; for example, to become a part of another culture). A crucial question for religious educators is, "How does one learn to speak and live one's faith in a world where many persons do not know the same stories or vocabulary and where their world views are very different from one's own?"

Words for the Journey

Once again, Brueggemann offers helpful insights into this dilemma as he reflects on an experience of the Israelites at the time when

King Hezekiah reigned in Judah and King Hoshea reigned in the northern kingdom of Israel (see 2 Kings 18–19). The king of Assyria sent troops to Jerusalem and threatened King Hezekiah. Rabshakeh, whom the king of Assyria sent, confronted the Israelites at the wall of the city and mocked them for putting trust in their king and their God. Hezekiah's representatives implored the Assyrians to speak to them in Aramaic, not in the language of Judah "in the hearing of the people" (2 Kings 18:26). But the Assyrians refused, for it was in their best interest to have all the people hear and understand their challenge: "Do not let Hezekiah deceive you, for he will not be able to deliver you out of my hand. Do not let Hezekiah make you rely on the Lord by saying, 'The Lord will surely deliver us, and this city will not be given into the hand of the king of Assyria' " (2 Kings 18:31). But the people did not answer, for their king had commanded that they put their faith in God. King Hezekiah was distraught and "tore his clothes, covered himself with sackcloth, and went into the house of the Lord" (2 Kings 19:1). Then he sent his intermediaries and the senior priests to consult the prophet Isaiah, who counseled them not to surrender and assured them that the Lord would indeed protect Jerusalem from the siege. It happened as the prophet had claimed, and the city was spared.

"People of faith must be bilingual," says Brueggemann. "They must have a public language for negotiation at the wall. And they must have a more communal language for processing behind the gate, in the community, out of sight and range of the imperial negotiators" (1989, p. 6). Language "behind the wall" is sectarian and reflects the story and life experiences of a particular community of faith. It is the language Isaiah used when the king's representatives came to hear a word from the Lord. It is true in a way that differs from the commonly accepted (dominant) view of reality. It is a necessary and vital language to know. However, persons who assume that their sectarian language is the only one, and hence the only truth, cut themselves off from engaging in life in the world. Language behind the wall is that of dreaming and visioning, "of remembering and hoping, of caring and fearing, of compassion and passion" (Brueggemann, 1989, p. 25). Sectarian language is valuable precisely because it can prepare people to engage in a critical and creative dialogue with the dominant culture to assess the way things are in light of the faith claims of their community.

On the other hand, "language at the wall" is the language of policy formation and negotiation. It is used to communicate with those who accept the dominant reading of reality. Individuals who have engaged in the discussions behind the wall and who are bilingual are now able to contribute to the public dialogue. Whereas conservatives may sometimes resist this language, liberals may run the risk of failing to remember the stories and ritual celebrations that must be told and experienced behind the wall and can thus thereby be subsumed by the dominant culture (Brueggemann, 1989, p. 25).

Adult religious education needs to prepare people to be bilingual. It should immerse them in the stories and rituals, the values and beliefs, of their particular faith community. That immersion leads to an alternative understanding of reality that honors the faith claims of the community to which they belong. At the same time adult religious education should help persons remain open to the language of the larger community so that they can hear and speak with understanding in that arena. As Mary Boys asserts, "Religious education requires the artistry of the sacramental imagination and the pragmatics of public service" (1989a, p. 180). Religious education has the task of teaching the stories, rituals, symbols, and values of the sectarian community (which takes place using the language behind the wall) so that it can "interface the dominant reading of reality freely, imaginatively, and critically" (Brueggemann, 1989, p. 13). The "artistry of the sacramental imagination" is learned and celebrated behind the wall, whereas "the pragmatics of public service" are discovered both behind and at the wall but are lived in the public arena.

There are significant metaphors in Jewish and Christian traditions that contribute to an understanding of the behind-the-wall language. The exodus is one. It conveys images of slavery and redemption, of faithfulness and unfaithfulness on the part of God's people, of promise and obedience, of God's faithfulness and gracious love. Out of the exodus experience comes the celebration of Passover—a time for teaching the very youngest children the story, for reminding all who they are and from where they came; a time for celebrating God's mighty act of liberation and God's promise that Elijah will return.

As scripture records, "When you come to the land that the Lord will give you, as [God] has promised, you shall keep this observance. And when your children ask you, 'What do you mean by this observance?' you shall say, 'It is the passover sacrifice to the Lord, for [God] passed over the houses of the Israelites in Egypt, . . . struck down the Egyptians but spared our houses.' And the people bowed down and worshipped" (Exod. 12:25-27).

For Christians, crucifixion-resurrection is a primary metaphor. It conveys images of sin and salvation, of death and life, of gift and responsibility. Out of a Christian understanding of Jesus' death and resurrection comes the celebration of eucharist—a time for rehearsing the story, for reminding all the people who and whose they are; a time for celebrating God's saving act and God's promise that the reign and realm of God is both present now and will be fulfilled in the future.

That rehearsal is powerfully stated in this eucharistic prayer as Christians from many traditions and nations gathered around the table at the World Council of Churches celebration in Lima, Peru and prayed:

> Almighty and Everlasting God, through your living Word you created all things, and pronounced them good. You made human beings in your own image, to share your life and reflect your glory. When the time had fully come, you gave Christ to us as the Way, the Truth and the Life. He accepted baptism and consecration as your Servant to announce the good news to the poor. At the last supper Christ bequeathed to us the eucharist, that we should celebrate the memorial of the cross and resurrection, and receive his presence as food. To all the redeemed Christ gave the royal priesthood and, in loving his brothers and sisters, chooses those who share in the ministry, that they may feed the Church with your Word and enable it to live by your Sacraments. Wherefore, Lord, with the angels and all the saints, we proclaim and sing your glory. . . . O God, Lord of the universe, you are holy and your glory is beyond measure. Upon your eucharist send the life-giving Spirit, who spoke by Moses and the Prophets, who overshadowed the Virgin Mary with grace, who descended upon Jesus in the river Jordan and upon the Apostles on the day of Pentecost. May

the outpouring of this Spirit of Fire transfigure this thanks-
giving meal that the bread and wine may become for us the
body and blood of Christ" [Thurian and Wainwright, 1983,
pp. 252–253].

This is the Christian story. It proclaims that those of us who
share in this language behind the wall and claim this story as our
own are recipients of this saving act of God. We are called to be
God's children. We are forgiven. We are free to live as faithful
servant leaders whose commission is "to do justice, and to love
kindness, and to walk humbly with [our] God" (Mic. 6:8b). The
Christian language behind the wall grows out of the experiences in
the Hebrew Bible, as well as in the New Testament, and our story
is understood (by Christians) as a continuation of the whole biblical
story.

The recovery of sectarian languages is much needed in our
day. With the recovery of the special stories of ethnic, gender, national, or religious groups can come a rediscovery of roots and a
new sense of "identity, energy and power" (Brueggemann, 1989,
p. 9). When people have a strong sense of who and whose they are,
they can be free to be open to those who are different. Fear cannot
hold persons in bondage if they are secure about their self-identity
and if they are connected to a community of persons who can
"speak their language" about life's deepest pains and promises. A
sense of superiority will not enslave persons who acknowledge that
the world is made up of many communities and that no one of them
has all the answers. Freed from fear and the need to hold the only
truth, persons in faith communities can seek ways to name and
claim their own stories and then find forums for using language at
the wall in order to contribute to the dialogue that will help make
this world a more just and hospitable place.

Education in communities of faith, Brueggemann claims,
should be concerned with developing both "the language of policy
formation and the language of transformative imagination" (1989,
p. 28). When faith communities engage in claiming the stories of
faith as their own, struggle with the prophetic word that threatens
to disrupt the status quo and to advocate for the poor and marginalized, and seek to discern and make sense of the meaning of death

and life, then they are well on their way to having fluent speakers of the language behind the wall. These speakers must be able to critique the state of their lives and families, their nation, and the world in light of the truth claims of their community of faith and to visualize ways to bring hope out of despair, justice out of oppression, love out of apathy and hate.

Once this is done, faith communities must be able to hear and speak the language at the wall as they seek to share their perspective on how policy ought to be developed and changed. In fact, people who enter the twenty-first century may really be called to be multilingual, for there is no longer only one language for the public forum. As we recognize the richness of many different cultures and acknowledge the complexity of the issues facing the global community, people may be called on to understand many kinds of communication as together they seek to create a public language where misunderstandings are minimized.

Ways of Knowing for the Journey

These ways of speaking require different ways of knowing. Knowledge should not be perceived as a given; rather, it results from a more active process of acting and reflecting, of relating and doing, of willing and being. Knowledge needs to be seen as fluid and relational.

For example, if we are to understand Christian religious education on the basis of a biblical model, it must be "grounded in a relational/experiential/reflective way of knowing that is informed by the Story of faith from Christians before us, and by the Vision toward which that Story points" (Groome, 1980, p. 145). Religious education is a way of knowing that holds past, present, and future in a creative tension. It holds that one cannot make clear delineations between content and process, as the two create a symbiotic relationship that changes both. This way of knowing is dynamic rather than static, creative rather than dogmatic, flexible rather than fixed. It can be discovered as one examines the journey of two followers of Jesus who leave Jerusalem following the crucifixion.

> Now on that same day two of them were going to a village called Emmaus, about seven miles from Jerusalem, and talk-

ing with each other about all these things that had happened. While they were talking and discussing, Jesus himself came near and went with them, but their eyes were kept from recognizing him. And he said to them, "What are you discussing with each other while you walk along?" They stood still, looking sad. Then one of them, whose name was Cleopas, answered him. "Are you the only stranger in Jerusalem who does not know the things that have taken place there in these days?" He asked them, "What things?" They replied, "The things about Jesus of Nazareth, who was a prophet mighty in deed and word before God and all the people, and how our chief priests and leaders handed him over to be condemned to death and crucified him. But we had hoped that he was the one to redeem Israel. Yes, and besides all this, it is now the third day since these things took place. Moreover, some women of our group astounded us. They were at the tomb early this morning, and when they did not find his body there, they came back and told us that they had indeed seen a vision of angels who said that he was alive. Some of those who were with us went to the tomb and found it just as the women had said; but they did not see him." Then he said to them, "Oh, how foolish you are, and how slow of heart to believe all that the prophets have declared! Was it not necessary that the Messiah should suffer these things and then enter into his glory?" Then beginning with Moses and all the prophets, he interpreted to them the things about himself in all the scriptures. As they came near the village to which they were going, he walked ahead as if he were going on. But they urged him strongly, saying, "Stay with us, because it is almost evening and the day is now nearly over." So he went in to stay with them. When he was at the table with them, he took bread, blessed and broke it, and gave it to them. Then their eyes were opened, and they recognized him; and he vanished from their sight. They said to each other, "Were not our hearts burning within us while he was talking to us on the road, while he was opening the scriptures to us?" That same hour they got up and returned to Jerusalem; and they found the eleven and their companions gathered together. They were saying, "The Lord has risen, indeed, and he has appeared to Simon!" Then they told what had happened on the road, and how he had been made known to them in the breaking of the bread" [Luke 24:13-35].

There are important clues to be found in this passage for those engaged in adult religious education. James Loder suggests that the transforming power of Christ's Spirit and that of the eucharist are at the heart of this account. In this encounter Christians discover that "convictional experiences are invitations or moments of awakening into a transparency that has been in the making for some time" (1989, p. 117–119). Convictional experiences take different forms, but they are equally important in other faith traditions.

One way of discerning the way adults learn is to examine this passage in light of Robert McAfee Brown's hermeneutical circle, or circle of interpretation (1984, pp. 21–28, 31). Some action in the world—in this case, Jesus' crucifixion—proves to be a very jarring experience that disrupts these disciples' way of making sense of their world. They are struggling with this discontinuity as they talk with one another on the road. "How are we going to make sense of what has happened?" they wonder. They acknowledge that they had apparently misjudged the situation when they tell the stranger, "We had hoped. . . ." When old ways of making sense no longer suffice, persons search for new forms that will take the current disruptions into account.

Persons of faith often turn to scripture with their just-formed questions to seek new answers. That is what Jesus offers as he recounts what the scriptures teach about who he is. As a result of hearing and reflecting in a different way, these two journeyers act: they invite this stranger to a meal. It is in the blessing and breaking of the bread that a fresh way of seeing is born. It turns their despair into joy and their broken dreams into hope. The danger of traveling from Emmaus to Jerusalem at night cannot restrain them from returning at once to Jerusalem to tell the other disciples what they have experienced. So it is that the circle is completed:

1. Action in the world challenges one's way of making meaning.
2. This challenge leads people to raise new questions as they reflect on how to make sense of life as it is being experienced.
3. They are now able to turn to an authoritative Word and hear it differently.
4. In response to the Word, they are challenged to act in new ways.
5. Finally, the arena in which they act widens as their world view is expanded. There is no end to the experiencing-questioning-reflecting-acting-experiencing—as life goes on!

Tad Guzie describes this process in a different way (1981, pp. 22-23). He suggests that the Emmaus passage in Luke offers a model for understanding both the sacraments and religious education. All learning begins with *raw experience;* in this case Jesus drew near and walked along with the two downhearted disciples. Much of life is made up of raw experience that provokes no reflection. But raw experience becomes *lived experience* when people think about it. In response to Jesus' question, "What things?", the two begin to share their experiences of pain and broken dreams. And lived experience can become *story.* In the Emmaus passage, it certainly does. Jesus began by reminding these two disciples of stories they already knew—stories about who Jesus was and what God called him to do. He broadened the scope so that the disciples could deal with their present experience in new ways. Story can also move us into *festivity,* and that is what happens here. It was in the taking, blessing, and breaking of bread—ritual acts that these disciples had shared with Jesus before as they celebrated the Passover together and as they experienced the sharing of the fish and loaves with the multitude—that "their eyes were opened, and they recognized him."

Ritual often becomes meaningless precisely because our celebrations have been cut off from the stories from which they came. One task, then, of religious education is to teach adults the stories of their faith community and to make the connections between them and their celebrations and rituals. This kind of insight can help adults make sense of their own life experiences.

Thomas Groome sees Luke 24:13-35 as a model for understanding ways of teaching and learning about faith (1980, pp. 135-136, 184-232). He suggests that the process begins when a *present activity* is named. In Luke there can be no doubt that this activity was to be found in the two disciples' conversation as they walk along the road. The second movement (the term Groome chooses because it conveys more fluidity than *stage*) takes place when people *tell their own stories* and reflect critically on how they relate to the present activity and what the consequences of their interpretation might be. In our example this opportunity arose when the rabbi who joined the two asks, "What things?" Only after the disciples had described how things were from their perspective and according to their experience and understanding did the yet-to-be-recognized

Jesus tell the story and vision that are found in scripture and have relevance to the life of the community. "Then beginning with Moses and all the prophets, he interpreted to them the things about himself in all the scriptures" (Luke 24:27). Once this Word has been offered, people need an opportunity to discover for themselves how the faith story *relates to their life situations*. In Luke that moment occurred when the disciples asked the stranger to join them for supper. It is interesting to note that Jesus still did not help them make the obvious connections. The familiar ritual act of breaking of bread revealed the truth. Their shattered world came together in new ways. Their vision *connected to that of Jesus* (Groome's fifth movement), and they were compelled to act.

Groome calls his five-movement process shared praxis. Reading his *Christian Religious Education* was a revelation to me because it made clear what I do when I am teaching most effectively. It is a process that can guide us as we engage in teaching and learning with adults in communities of faith.

Feeding Those Who Journey in Faith

These models of Brown, Guzie, and Groome, which are based on how Jesus interacted with two distraught disciples, suggest that there may be an underlying way human beings have of learning—that is, of making sense out of the life experiences and the situations that they encounter and of discovering ways to respond that create satisfaction and hope rather than pain and despair.

Learning is a natural and basic human activity. There is great hunger in our day for learning that will give purpose and meaning to life. That is the hunger that Jesus recognized when he ignored his disciples' pleas to send the crowd away; instead, he fed the five thousand. That is the hunger that communities of faith have the potential for satisfying. Adult religious educators can provide resources and processes to enable their communities to fulfill this need.

People who are contented with their lives are not very hungry. Those who want and need feeding generally have

1. A disruption in their lives: there are questions and perplexities that need attention. Raw experience is becoming lived ex-

perience, and there is a present situation that they are ready to address.

2. A need to reflect on their own experiences: there are stories to be told (and retold) and new questions to be pursued. This is the time of exploration.

3. New ears for hearing the scriptures: these people are ready to look to the past with a readiness to hear old words in new ways to help in the present.

4. New eyes for seeing connections between personal stories and the faith story: these are connections that compel individuals to move beyond seeing to acting. This is revelation (a new way of seeing) that leads to a reflective-active dialogue that leaves little room for those who would observe from the sidelines.

5. A desire to celebrate through remembering and ritualizing: once the Story is owned, it must be celebrated. Passover and eucharist demonstrate this truth in profound ways. But celebrating can never stand alone; otherwise, it is empty and lifeless. If it is to be authentic, celebrating must be preceded by owning the Story and followed by acting on it.

6. A commitment to serve: having received insight, grace, understanding, and hope, persons *must* act. Authentic celebration and service are inseparable.

This way of understanding teaching and learning can provide a model for discipleship that can be visualized as an interactive process that includes the six aspects listed above. It is a process that is in constant motion. It is like a hologram in that the angle and the amount of light affect how and what one sees, and there are always other angles and new perspectives to be grasped. There is not one logical progression; the puzzle of life can be approached in many different ways.

This approach to adult religious education offers possibilities for new life. As Loder observes, "Conflict embraced and borne with expectancy . . . is not yet overwhelming . . . because the possibility of new being, however marginal, stubbornly persists, offering the hope of transformation in the midst of an otherwise hopeless situation" (1989, p. 100).

Life is a journey—for the individual as well as for communities of faith, nations, and the global community. Islam's origin, like Christianity's, began as a captive people sought deliverance and experienced hope offered by God (see Cox, 1988a, pp. 20-44). Faith communities are born when disruptions require persons to ask different and varied questions and to seek new perspectives that they feel compelled to celebrate and to share with others.

This process is illustrated by Marianne Sawicki, who examines "the gospel's travel from mouth to mouth, heart to heart, among ordinary Christians" in her book *The Gospel in History: Portrait of a Teaching Church* (1988, p. 6). She finds in the gospels a "basic pattern of discipleship—experience, share, and follow Jesus until death." This pattern provides a way of living the Christian life that embodies "caring for people's needs and celebrating both God's recklessly forgiving love of the people and the people's brotherly and sisterly relationship with one another. . . . [Jesus'] message takes effort through the combined impact of *care, celebration* and *call"* (1988, p. 62—emphasis mine). Although Sawicki is speaking from a Christian perspective, these three c's may offer a way of understanding the faith journey of persons outside Christian communities.

In Buddhism, for example, *sangha* seems to relate to friendship (care) and to the concept of a covenant people who find courage to embark on the journey because of Buddha (call); *dharma* may be understood as "a search for an unaffected and honest encounter with all one meets—with nature, other people, and the self" (celebration) (Cox, 1988a, pp. 74-95). Huston Smith describes Buddhism's three vows in this way: "I take refuge in the *Buddha*—the fact that there was an explorer who made this trip and proved to us that it is possible. I take refuge in the *dharma*, the vehicle of transport, this boat to which we have committed our lives in the conviction that it is seaworthy. I take refuge in the *sangha*, the Order, the crew that is navigating this trip and in whom we have confidence. The shoreline of the world has been left behind; until we set foot on the further bank, these are the only things in which we can trust" (Smith, 1958, p. 154).

The call often comes as the result of a disruption—Moses was a fugitive from Egypt where he was wanted for murder when God called him to go back to Egypt to tell the Pharaoh to let the Hebrew slaves (on whom their economy rested) go. If it does not come at a time of disruption, the call often causes disorder: Peter had to leave fishing as a way of life and means of supporting his family to become a traveling student in a not-always-popular rabbi's school. Persons who hear the call from God are good candidates for learning.

Care has much to do with naming and reflecting on one's own experience and empathizing with the experiences of others. It means being willing to change both what one understands and what one does.

Celebration entails naming, claiming, and sharing experiences that make a difference to who we are and who we are becoming. Celebration in communities of faith is both a claiming of gift and an empowering of possibility. It is the joining of festivity and a renewed commitment to discipleship.

So it is that we are all in the midst of a journey. It is a journey that involves others. In its broadest sense, it is one that is dependent on the state of well-being or dis-ease of all God's children and of all creation.

All persons learn on the journey. What they learn and how they choose to act on it varies. And everyone needs food for the journey. At times, it seems that there is not enough to go around. Some believe and act as if it were hopeless to expect to be loved or to find meaning and purpose in life. They ignore the hunger pangs because they are convinced that there is no food available to them; they give up. Others strike out in anger or frustration to fill the void they feel.

Persons in faith communities have food to share; both Passover and eucharist are symbols of that fact. Jews and Christians have clear commissions to feed the hungry. Muslims also have such a commission. In the Koran we find, "Would that you knew what the Height is! It is the freeing of someone in bondage, the feeding, in the day of famine, of an orphan or needy person in distress, to have faith and encourage one another, in perseverance and mercy" (Sura 90).

In the Hebrew scriptures we read, "Mortal, prophesy against the shepherds of Israel: prophesy and say to them—to the shepherds: Thus says the Lord God: Ah, you shepherds of Israel who have been feeding yourselves! Should not shepherds feed the sheep? You eat the fat, you clothe yourselves with the wool, you slaughter the fat-lings; but you do not feed the sheep. You have not strengthened the weak, you have not healed the sick, you have not bound up the injured, you have not brought back the strayed, you have not sought the lost, but with force and harshness you have ruled them" (Ezek. 34:2-4).

After the resurrected Jesus had breakfast with his disciples on the lake shore, "Jesus said to Simon Peter, 'Simon son of John, do you love me more than these?' He said to him, 'Yes, Lord; you know that I love you'. Jesus said to him, 'Feed my lambs'. A second time he said to him, 'Simon, son of John, do you love me?' He said to him, 'Yes, Lord, you know that I love you'. Jesus said to him. 'Tend my sheep'. He said to him a third time, 'Simon, son of John, do you love me?' And he said to him, 'Lord, you know everything; you know that I love you'. Jesus said to him, 'Feed my sheep'" (John 21:15b-17). Again, "If your enemies are hungry, give them bread to eat; and if they are thirsty, give them water to drink" (Prov. 25:21; also see Rom. 12:20).

There is a clear call to Jews, Christians, and Muslims to feed the hungry. The food that is required is both physical and spiri-tual—depending on the needs of those who come. Often it is both.

Our world and our communities of faith are full of hunger-ing people. Adult religious education can bring gifts that the com-munity can share. The need and planning for this banquet will now be the focus of our attention. Journeys are often more productive and more satisfying when they are shared. You are invited to join with me as we look at issues of life and faith that provide the context for our journeys.

TWO

How
Religious Education
Nourishes
Life and Faith

[One] drops but a pebble into the one great lake of life, and
the ripples spread to unguessed shores, to congeal into a
pattern even in the timeless skies of night.
—*Frank Waters, 1942, p. 266*

"It just doesn't make sense!" he exclaimed. "I can't understand it!"
she responded. "What can we do?" they lamented. When the ways
we think or act no longer make sense in terms of our understandings
about who we are or in relation to the world in which we find
ourselves, we experience cognitive dissonance. We have to find new
ways of thinking and doing that are appropriate to our life situations. We may even have to find new ways of speaking—creating a
new vocabulary and new metaphors, for it is clear that "language
influences the way we think and that language is in turn shaped by
the culture of the speakers. . . . Language, culture, and thought are
dynamically interrelated" (Russell, 1987, p. 45).

Many people in our time can identify with Celie in Alice
Walker's *The Color Purple*. Celie discovers that she is no longer

able or willing to write letters to God, whom she has come to experience and understand as both white and male (Walker, 1982, pp. 164–166).

Today, Western, predominantly hierarchical, patriarchal ways of thinking and speaking block many people's ability to hear and relate to God. Perhaps as many as two-thirds of the people of our world suffer deprivation and are oppressed, do not have access to adequate housing, food, and employment, to quality education and medical care, and to structures that have power to both maintain and change the way things are. These people cry out for a faith that speaks to them where they are. It is to them that faith communities must both listen and speak. Sallie McFague suggests that religious-theological language in our day must face the issue of the idolatry of language, which leads to literalism, and of irrelevance, which leads persons who are seeking to find answers and make meaning away from the faith communities to which they belong (1982, p. 193). If our old ways of thinking and speaking about God and faith do not work, can we find new and more varied ones that speak with authenticity to individual life situations and still remain faithful to the living God? I believe that adult religious education can provide us with ways of engaging in this life-saving task.

Seeing in a Mirror, Dimly

People deal with cognitive dissonance in a variety of ways. They sometimes deny their experience and cling to the old ways of thinking and doing. That alternative is more attractive if they can find a community of like-minded persons who will join in the denying process. Some religious communities take this road.

Another approach is to seek to stay on the same road but to make some unavoidable changes. Many main-line (old-line) faith communities are choosing this road today.

Some persons and communities look for a fork in the road and make major changes in how they think and act; however, they carry much of the baggage from their previous way of being, and some of it continues to be useful. Vatican II may have been a catalyst for this kind of change in the Roman Catholic church.

Some, changing direction completely, experience conversion—a 180-degree turn! They now need a different map, and they may find different companions for the journey. Paul had this kind of experience on the road to Damascus (see Acts 9:1–22).

Still others give up. They refuse to continue on the journey, or they strike out with no sense of direction or purpose. Hedonism, drug or alcohol addiction, workaholism, mental illness, and suicide are examples of how people may refuse to face cognitive dissonance and the demands of the journey.

But another road exists. Persons can choose to seek to work and live in harmony with the whole created order. When they do, their need to build and maintain walls will decrease. There may be a renewed energy to invest in the journey as they come to know better and trust more their companions; this openness will also bring new companions with whom they can share and learn. Paradigms will shift, and new frameworks will emerge that allow for "multiple authorities to enrich, rather than to outrank one another" (Russell, 1987, p. 33).

More and more often, persons are confronted with events and circumstances that strain a theology beyond its ability to cope. Instead of isolating themselves from these anomalies in order to hang on to their faith or giving up on theology (and God?) as a way of coping with pressure, people have the option to expand and complement the traditional models—a process that allows them to incorporate conflicting or new data so that it can be incorporated into their theological understandings. This process requires discovering appropriate images and meaningful language with which to express and name this new way of understanding faith (McFague, 1982, pp. 140–141).

This last option can only happen, however, if we are willing to risk stepping outside our own way of understanding for a time—to visit another world by "leap[ing] out from our shell of absolute certainty and construct[ing] a whole new world based on some other person's ideas of 'reality,' other assumptions of 'truths'" (Daloz, 1986, p. 228). This does not mean that we become chameleon-like; nor does it mean that it does not matter what we believe or do. We simply must acknowledge that none of us has the whole truth; what we believe and value has been formed in large part by the time and place and circumstances of our birth, by our life experiences, and by the communities of which we have been a part. Stepping into another world may sometimes make us more committed to our own views. But we will have more understanding and compassion than if we had refused to test our own beliefs.

Most adults have already engaged in this process at those times when deeply held values and important relationships have come into conflict. Parents experience this dilemma when their children make choices that reflect different values and life-styles. A powerful example comes from *Fiddler on the Roof*, when Tevye is torn between his faith in God and his deep love for his daughter, Chava, who begs him to accept her and her gentile husband. He laments: "Accept them? How can I accept them? Can I deny everything I believe in? On the other hand, can I deny my own child? On the other hand, how can I turn my back on my faith, my people? If I try to bend that far, I will break. On the other hand . . ." (Stein, 1964, p. 103). Sometimes we come down on one side of the issue, sometimes on another. Sometimes we may find ways to reframe the questions and discover alternative approaches that we could not have imagined so long as we were bound by our old questions. But we must keep in mind that human truth is not absolute.

As Paul reminds us, "For now we see in a mirror, dimly, but then we will see face to face. Now I know only in part; then I will know fully, even as I have been fully known" (1 Cor. 13:12). If the God in whom we trust is truth, then no question is beyond asking, and other viewpoints can be heard and examined. We must never forget that we, like Robert McAfee Brown, have often "filtered information carefully to make sure that nothing threatened [our basic] convictions" (1980, p. 54). When we uncritically accept the perspective created by our experiences, as if it were absolute truth, we may be putting up roadblocks as the Spirit of God seeks to lead us on our journey. The ideologies that form the basis of our lives (often unconsciously or uncritically) might "be compared to the water in which fish swim; it is so much a part of our ordering environment that we do not even recognize its existence, to say nothing of its dominating power" (Evans, Evans, and Kennedy, 1987, p. 268).

Lest the task of receiving and making meaning of life and death overwhelm us, we need to remember that all any of us can do is to begin from wherever we are. In the map of life, we need to find a starting point and just put one foot in front of the other as we seek to grow in knowing and doing God's will. For Christians, Jesus Christ provides the clue to reality; for Jews, it is the Torah—broadly conceived to include both written and oral tradition; for Muslims, it is the Koran. But we must not forget that these are only clues and that there is, in a sense, "absolute relativeness" (Jenkins, 1990, pp. 80-91).

Whenever we accept data and doctrine as absolute, we ignore the personal and relational aspect of knowing truth. One of the reasons the pharisees and scribes were so frustrated with Jesus is that relationships and individual needs took precedence for him over law and doctrine. Jesus healed on the sabbath, talked with Samaritan women, and ate with tax collectors and prostitutes.

Of course, there are hazards in ignoring data and doctrine. It is possible to lose one's roots and one's sense of past, present, and future within a community of faith if one focuses solely on present relationships to the neglect of one's faith story, traditions, and beliefs.

As Parker Palmer says, "In truthful knowing we neither infuse the world with our subjectivity (as premodern knowing did) nor hold it at arm's length manipulating it to suit our needs (as is the modern style). In truthful knowing the knower becomes coparticipant in a community of faithful relationships with other persons and creatures and things, with whatever our knowledge makes known. We find truth by pledging our troth, and knowing becomes a reunion of separated beings whose primary bond is not of logic but of love" (1983, p. 32).

Jesus made this point clear when he assured those who believed in him, "If you continue in my word, you are truly my disciples; and you will know the truth, and the truth will make you free" (John 8:32). Truth is much more than beliefs or doctrine. It is relational and communal.

Truth frees Christians to live as followers of one who understood his mission to be to "bring good news to the poor, . . . proclaim release to the captives, and recovery of sight to the blind, to let the oppressed go free, to proclaim the year of the Lord's favor" (Luke 4:18b-19; see also Isa. 61:1-2). Truth empowers Jews to "do what is just, to show constant love, and to live in humble fellowship with our God" (Mic. 6:8). Truth inspires followers of Baha u'llah to work toward his admonition "O rich ones on earth! The poor in your midst are My trust; guard ye My trust" (inscribed above an entrance of the Baha'i House of Worship in Willmette, Illinois).

Truth cannot be understood apart from living in harmony with all God's children and the whole creation. For Christians faithful discipleship requires participation in the body of Christ, the community of faith. Jews' self-understanding as God's chosen people brings both promise and responsibility as they seek to live as partners and faithful followers of Yahweh.

By stepping outside a dominant culture and into that of the Pueblo Indians, we may be able to see more clearly the absolute relativity we have been seeking to discern. Frank Waters portrays a meeting of the council of elders:

> Let us move evenly, together, brothers.
> A young man went into the mountains. He killed a deer out of season. He got arrested, and a knock on the head to boot. He will have to pay a fine, doubtless, for disobeying those Government laws we have sworn to uphold with our canes of office. A simple matter.
> But wait, Was it so simple?
> This young man was an Indian, born in our pueblo, belonging to our tribe. Or was he, properly speaking? There was the definition of an Indian by the Government—so much Indian blood, land ownership, all that. But there was the definition of an Indian by the Council according to his conformance to custom, tradition, his participation in ceremonials. Now this young man has been lax, very lax; we have warned him. He has disobeyed us; we have punished him. And now he has disobeyed the laws of the Government outside, likewise. What have we to do with this, that we should interfere?
> Now there is this. There are good Indians among us, and there are those who look under their eyes. But we are all in one nest. No Indian is an individual. He is a piece of the pueblo, the tribe. Is it proper to consider that we have done wrong against the Government, our white father, betrayed our canes of office?
> Yet there was this to consider. All this land was ours—the mountain, the valleys, the desert, Indian land. We have the papers to it from the Spanish King. The Mexicans came, the white people—the gringos. They built themselves a town on our land, Indian land. We got nothing for it. Now when the

Spanish King opened his hand, Our Father at Washington
closed his own hand upon the land. He told us, "You will be
paid for it. The day will come with compensation." What did
we want with money? We wanted land, our land, Indian land.
But mostly we wanted the mountains. We wanted the mountains, our mother, between whose breasts lies the little blue eye
of faith. The deep turquoise lake of life. Our lake, our church.
Where we make our pilgrimages, hold our ceremonials. . . .
Now what is this? We have waited. The day of compensation
has not come. The mountains are Government forests. Not
ours. The Mexicans pasture their sheep and goats upon the
slopes. *Turistas* scatter paper bags unseemly upon the ground.
They throw old fish bait into our sacred lake. Government
men, these rangers, ride through it at will. Is any man safe?
Look at this one's broken head. Will our ceremonials long be
inviolate from foreign eyes? Now, then is it we who are injured
and must seek reparation, demand our rights, our mountains?
This is what I say. God knows, will help us, will give us
strength.
The voices kept creeping around the room . . . .
In the government office two hundred miles away there is
that Indian lawyer, our mouth in many matters. There is the
judge in town, a short walk. Are we to turn this young man
alone over to the judge? Or are we to call this Indian lawyer?
And what are we to tell him? We must move evenly together.
We must be one mind, one heart, one body. Silence spoke,
and it spoke the loudest of all [1942, pp. 22–23, reprinted
with the permission of The Ohio University Press/Swallow
Press, Athens].

The elders portrayed in this council understand the dynamic and
symbiotic relationships that foster healing of body and soul, those
of the created world and history, and those between and among the
communities of the world. They understand that wholeness requires community and silence and struggling to see every side of
experience. One's growing toward wholeness may be centered in
faith in a compassionate and just God who acts in history to save
all creation. Justice and love become the guiding norms as persons
of faith seek to make sense of life and death. But justice and love
must be embodied in communities and in all of life's relationships,
even as they are embodied in those who speak prophetic words of
judgment and hope as messengers of the Transcendent. What that
means—and how that is to be experienced and shared—depends on
context. For Jews, as we have noted, Torah is the key. For Chris-

tians, the way of discerning justice and love most fully is offered through a relationship with God through Jesus Christ. For Buddhists and Hindus a key may be an avatar—one among many who embodies the ultimate (Cox, 1988a, p. 89).

There are no easy or fixed answers. As Palmer says, a knowing "that springs from love will implicate us in the web of life; it will wrap the knower and the known in compassion, in a bond of awesome responsibility as well as transforming joy; it will call us to involvement, mutuality, accountability" (1983, p. 9). It humbles us because we recognize that the ripples from our pebbles go far beyond anything that we intend or imagine.

Nearly five decades after the appearance of Frank Waters's book about Pueblo culture, the scientific community was shaken by Stephen Jay Gould's *Wonderful Life: The Burgess Shale and the Nature of History*. He calls into question a long-accepted classification schema and interpretation of fossils from the Burgess shale in the Canadian Rockies. The book is as much about ways of knowing as it is about paleontology. Gould, who teaches biology, geology, and the history of science at Harvard University, asserts that our "conceptual blinders can preclude observation" (1989, p. 128) and that "biases, preferences, social values, and psychological attitudes [and I would add, theological beliefs] all play a strong role in the process of discovery. . . . Science, as actually practiced, is a complex dialogue between data and preconceptions" (p. 244). Whenever we find ourselves being confronted with a dualistic, linear framework that would appear to dictate a choice between two extremes or acceptance of a position on the continuum between them, it is time to move away from that line and seek to discern alternative perspectives that offer a variety of ways of posing the problem and creating possible solutions (Gould, 1989, p. 51).

Abraham Heschel, a Jewish rabbi, offers this principle as a guide to knowing truth. It is, he says, the recognition that we must "know what we see rather than to see what we know" (1962, vol. 1, p. xi). Perhaps when Jesus joined the two who were walking and talking on the road to Emmaus and the text says, "Their eyes were kept from recognizing him" (Luke 24:16), it is really saying that these two were *seeing* what they *knew*. It is only in the blessing and breaking of the bread at table that "their eyes were opened and they recognized him" (Luke 24:31); at this point they *knew* what they *saw*.

As James Ashbrook points out, "We are ever making sense of our senses by stating what they mean. We cannot 'not' interpret what we observe and experience. . . . Memory involves taking highly organized and emotionally significant information into a sense of the continuity of reality. . . . we select information, sort it, filter it, incorporate it according to whether it is interesting and pleasurable or dangerous and painful, to be approached or to be avoided" (1989, pp. 19–20). Making meaning is dependent on our memories. We cannot imagine a future without remembering our past. Our sense of identity (who and whose we are), our personal and communal stories, and all that gives life meaning are bound up in our gift of memory. *Soul* is the term Ashbrook uses to identify "our unique personality and our capacity for centered decisions, initiative, and wholeness" (1989, p. 25). For persons of faith, at least, sculpting meaning and nourishing the soul are integrally bound together.

Nourishing the soul is a process that involves us in finding "our true self in an ever-widening circle, first in the whole and then in God" (Jones, 1985, p. 187). It is a lifelong process that leads toward "solidarity with others" so that we have moved beyond the state of being undifferentiated, as infants are with their mothers, become able to break free from the confines of family and small groups that may enslave us, and grow toward an inclusive wholeness (Jones, 1985, pp. 186–188). Those who choose to engage in soul-nourishing are working toward claiming the promise that though "now we see in a mirror, dimly, . . . then we will see face to face. Now [we] know only in part; then [we] will know fully, even as [we] have been fully known. And now faith, hope, and love abide, these three; and the greatest of these is love" (1 Cor. 13:12–13).

"The Nations Are in an Uproar, the Kingdoms Totter!" (Ps. 46:6a)

The state of nations and the world today is tenuous at the very best. The steady arms buildup continues to create poverty, which is already at epidemic levels. The effectiveness of all social institutions—including governments, schools, faith communities, and families—is being challenged by technologies that have galloped ahead of our ability to make ethical decisions about them; by upheavals in work and leisure; by demands from the marginalized for more power, which are reflected in changing views of authority; and by sudden political and economic shifts.

Environmental crises are symptoms of a world whose existence is being threatened by our own technology and consumer lifestyles. Global warming, the destruction of rain forests, oil spills, radiation poisoning, overburdened land fills, the depletion of nonrenewable natural resources, the loss of top soil, and the poisoning of our water and air are signs that cannot be ignored or seen in isolation. "The times cry out for a dramatic change in our relationship to our neighbor, to the earth, and, at root, to God" (Wallis, 1983, p. 17).

The threat of nuclear destruction—whether through a desperate act of war or terrorism or by accident—exacts a price on both national economies and individual psyches. The social diseases of racism, classism, sexism, and ageism also take their tolls.

The increasing population, coupled with a growing gap between the poor and the rich, increases the threat of social destruction by the disenfranchised who are less and less willing to be controlled by oppressive institutions. We would do well to heed these words: "The truth tends to upset a lot of things. . . . let us listen to the victims, the hurting, the oppressed, as they tell us how the world looks through their eyes, and especially how the United States looks through their eyes" (Brown, 1980, p. 112).

There are no quick fixes. We compartmentalize and ignore these issues to our own and the whole human family's peril. "The entire creation is groaning, singing, slurping, slithering, sobbing, oozing with . . . life! But we are pushing it toward death" (Raines, 1984, p. 144).

The state of many families and individuals is also at risk. The global picture is the macrocosm; there is little comfort to be found when we shift our attention to the microcosm. It may be sobering to discover the circumstances of people you know and care about, as I did recently in a seminary class on educational ministry with families. What I found is that these thirty-one adults, including students from five different seminaries in the Chicago area and several interested laypersons from local congregations, were undergoing personal stresses related to broken or blended families; parenting issues; step-parenting; aging parents with failing health or financial problems; a variety of addictions—drugs, alcohol, gambling, work; children or parents who were struggling with their identity as homosexuals; AIDS, cancer, or terminal illnesses; unemployment or underemployment; dual-career or commuter marriages; retirement or uprootedness; the death of loved ones; broken relationships; family members in prison; and bankruptcy. The list goes on and on and on; you can no doubt add to it from your own experiences.

These stresses are real. They do not respect age, gender, race, nationality, class, or religion. The pressures on individuals and families that have access to resources and power are very great. These strains are compounded for those in war-torn regions, in areas of extreme drought, and in neighborhoods or nations where social upheaval and rapid social change may be coupled with poverty and inadequate social services, including health care and education.

Even in the developed nations there are people who are tantalized by goods and services that are totally beyond their reach. Their own poverty, joblessness, homelessness, or hunger adds to their sense of anger and despair. These people are likely to explode in unpredictable times and places.

How are we to respond to the seemingly overwhelming obstacles to wholeness for persons, nations, and the earth? Does religious education hold a key? Can we claim the psalmist's faith that "by awesome deeds you answer us with deliverance, O God of our salvation; you are the hope of all the ends of the earth and of the farthest seas" (Ps. 65:5)?

We must accept the truth that "the means that we utilize in pursuit of various ends are a spiritual window into our own souls. This is as true for nations [and faith communities] as for individuals" (Nelson-Pallmeyer, 1989, p. 59). Both the content and processes of our responses require careful, prayerful attention.

What does one's faith (Jewish, Christian, Muslim, Baha'i, Buddhist, Hindu, indigenous religion, new religion) offer to persons who are seeking to make sense of their lives and world? Religious educators are called upon to broaden their understanding of education so that human beings are encouraged to discover "how meanings are made in culture" and also "to empower people to function as receivers and creators of meaning" (Seymour, O'Gorman, and Foster, 1984, p. 119). As a primary institution for creating meaning, the faith community's educational ministry can be an agent of social transformation.

Theologizing as a Spiritual Discipline

Theology has been described as "the studied expression of faith" that takes place from within the faith community and yet requires "some stepping-back, or objectivity, a seeking after clarity and coherence and an application of reason to faith" (Moore, 1983, pp. 68–69). Theology must "sink its roots into a faith lived in ecclesial communion" (Boys, 1989a, p. 201). It is the work of all the people of God and cannot be confined to the classroom or to scholars.

That work can be greatly enhanced by the conscious use of a variety of metaphors. The metaphor—"one of the oldest, most deeply embedded, even indispensable ways of knowing in the history of human consciousness"—offers ways to take qualities of a known and gain insight into the unknown (Apps, 1985, pp. 38–39). Metaphors generate questions and underlie our theories and our theologies. Sometimes their use is unconscious. When they are, they can influence us unknowingly (Sternberg, 1990, pp. 3–19). For example, when teachers speak about faith using metaphors of war— battle, victory, and the conquering of sin—they may communicate more than they intend. They may be fostering images of winners and losers that overshadow images of inclusivity and care.

As nothing we say about that reality that "transcends human experience" can claim to be absolutely true, our theologizing about God must rely on "metaphors from human experience" (Maitland, 1985, p. 50). Gordon Kaufman claims that "this metaphorical aspect of God-talk" is "the primary work of theology" (Kaufman, 1981, p. 11). Metaphors can illuminate and can create questions for discovering the mystery and meaning of death and life. Exploring a variety of metaphors frees us to examine many different ways of understanding who God is and who God calls us to be.

One of the grave dangers in faith communities is that theology becomes rigid. Too often we fail to engage in dynamic processes that draw on our past (both communal and personal); we fail to act on our hopes for the future, based on our experiences that God is faithful and keeps promises; and we are then unable to seek to understand and live faithfully in the present. We may find ourselves being handed old interpretations of experiences from the past as God's truth for us now and for all time. God is most assuredly *not* dead, but there is little life in secondhand doctrine that is not examined and claimed as one's own. Seeing metaphors as reality instead of as concepts or images that point us toward reality leads to lifeless, dogmatic faith.

Because we live in a world that is threatened on every side, there is a longing on the part of many persons for authoritative religious statements and simple moral solutions that they can cling to in order to feel safe. The giving and receiving of fixed answers is a futile attempt both to protect people from questions they do not want to face and to preserve the power of those in authority and the status quo (Jenkins, 1990, pp. 114–118).

"Talk about God (theo-logy) comes after the silence of prayer and after commitment," claims Gustavo Gutierrez (1984, p. 136). Christians, the body of Christ, are called into a ministry of work with the poor and oppressed, of deep caring, of sharing and prayer; in this way it is possible to recover the faith of Abraham who, "by faith, . . . obeyed when he was called . . . and he set out, not knowing where he was going" (Heb. 11:8). David Jenkins affirms Gutierrez's claim when he says, "Our emergent theology, . . . must be open theology, must be *broken* theology. . . . And in this connection we have to be quite clear that it is impossible to do theology apart from a spiritual discipline which is related to worship and prayer" (1990, p. 158).

Theology can be authentic only when it is grounded—when it has a home. Theology is practiced within particular cultures at specific times. It has meaning precisely because it speaks to people about their past experiences, present existence, and future hopes. It is for this reason that this book on adult religious education often uses and builds on metaphors from the Christian faith. As a Christian, I speak from that perspective, though I also try to be open to the truth that persons of other faith traditions offer to the dialogue.

This position assumes that we cannot take into ourselves theology from other cultures and times without examining it; testing it against our history, experiences, and hopes; and reappropriating it in ways that make sense for our present lives and faith communities. Likewise, those in other cultures and faiths cannot take what we can offer without undertaking this same process.

The priest in Shusaku Endo's powerful novel, *Silence,* set in the sixteenth and seventeenth centuries when Christianity was forbidden in Japan, failed to understand that there is no such thing as a pure, culture-free faith. This broken priest, who under torture had renounced his faith, tells one of his former students who also finally apostatized: " . . . in the churches we built throughout this country the Japanese were not praying to the Christian God. They twisted God to their own way of thinking in a way we can never imagine. . . . No. That is not God. It is like a butterfly caught in a spider's web. At first it is certainly a butterfly, but the next day only the externals, the wings and the trunk, are those of a butterfly; it has lost its true reality and has become a skeleton. In Japan our God is just like that butterfly caught in the spider's web; only the exterior form of God remains, but it has already become a skeleton. . . . They did not believe in the Christian God. . . . The Japanese till this day have never had the concept of God; and they never will" (1969, pp. 240–241).

One task, then, is to understand the metaphors that have been used by others, to adopt them because they speak to us with power today, or to find other metaphors that help us in relating to God, who is inclusive, all-embracing, justice-seeking love. Metaphors offer a dynamic way of nourishing the soul, where persons may encounter the living God and come to know and understand in light of their own past and present and as they move toward their hopes for the future.

Metaphors, says McFague, see "one thing as something else, pretending 'this' is 'that' because we do not know how to think or talk about 'this', so we use 'that' as a way of saying something about it. Thinking metaphorically means spotting a thread of similarity between two dissimilar objects, events, or whatever, one of which is better known than the other, and using the better-known one as a way of speaking about the lesser known" (1982, p. 15). Metaphorical thinking is a part of our ordinary, everyday way of thinking and being and communicating. It allows us to begin with what we know and move toward knowing the unknown.

For Christians Jesus' parables, when taken all together, help us glimpse the power and the peace that is available in the metaphor of the kingdom or reign and rule of God. The kingdom or rule of God, McFague maintains, became a dominant metaphor that she believes is "the root metaphor" of Christianity. Dominant metaphors become models. Models can serve as mediators when people move from metaphors toward conceptual thought. A model can function as a filter: people understand a less familiar subject in light of its similarities with a more familiar subject (1982, p. 23).

Models are both necessary and dangerous. We cannot make meaning without them, for they enable us to see holistically; but they can encourage idolatrous thinking by claiming *to be* that to which they point or insisting that the metaphor captures the whole truth about what it represents (see McFague, 1982, pp. 14–29). Metaphors can be keys to many and varied images of God and faith and discipleship. Theological (conceptual) language that moves us beyond metaphors to a more generalized level of discourse must remain in a symbiotic relationship with metaphorical language so that "images 'feed' concepts [and] concepts 'discipline' images. Images without concepts are blind; concepts without images are sterile. . . . Images are never free of the need for interpretation by concepts, their critique of competing images, or their demythologizing of literalized models. Concepts are never free of the need for funding by images, the affectional and existential richness of images, and the qualification against conceptual pretensions supplied by the plurality of images" (McFague, 1982, p. 26).

Now is a time to examine old metaphors about God and faith and to be open to new ones (or newly recovered metaphors from our own faith traditions). Biblical metaphors that may be recovered include God as rock and mother hen and lover. To be open, listen, and learn from others' experiences of God in their lives does not mean that we are compromising truth as we have experienced it. "But truth is very elusive. . . . We are more likely to catch glimpses of truth when we allow what we think and believe to be tested. Truth does not seem to flourish when imprisoned in rigid dogmatic statements or in an infallible teaching authority. It seems to prefer the company of persons from all walks of life. Let us be clear, then, that it is not our business to protect the truth. Rather it is our business to serve the truth wherever and whenever it is found" (Song, 1987, p. 15).

Rabbi Irving Greenberg is reported to have offered this working principle for the future: " 'No statement, theological or otherwise, should be made that would not be credible in the presence of burning children' " (Brown, 1980, p. 127). Theology must face, in truth, who we have been and are, as well as who God calls us to be. Theology needs to be ongoing; it is born of our experiencing and reflecting, our feeling and thinking, our hoping and acting. The experiential base out of which theology is born must be expanded to include all of God's creation and must try to be especially open to the truths reflected in the experiences of the poor and marginalized. For example, we in the United States have had to broaden our understanding of the basic assertion, "All men are created equal," to include slaves, women, all nationalities, and gays. Scripture (which has been interpreted and domesticated to a great extent by dominant Western cultures) offers "good news to the poor," as followers of the gospel "turn the world upside down" (Acts 17:6); it offers "a new heaven and a new earth" (Rev. 21:1; see also Isa. 65:17, 66:22). Finally, it may become clear that for *all* of God's people— "our deepest and longest interests are mutual" (Raines, 1984, p. 134).

Some Metaphors for Those Who Journey in Faith in Our Day

There are some powerful metaphors that seem to be relevant to persons who seek to journey in faith in our day. Metaphors are food that nourish our souls. They provide us with language for the journey. They introduce questions and encourage us to explore issues and ideas. Metaphors emerge from cultures, from faith traditions, and from the times. I will examine several that may speak powerfully to Christians at the dawn of a new century. Those of other traditions are invited to explore these and other metaphors that may be helpful.

Kingdom of God. As we have seen, one metaphor that may speak to Christians is *kingdom* or *reign and realm of God.* God's ultimate purpose for all creation is reflected in Jesus' teaching, preaching, and healing ministry and in his death and resurrection. It is a gift that calls us into relationship with God, each other, and all creation that is to be lived through faithful discipleship so that all creation might be redeemed (Groome, 1980, pp. 49–51). Sister Mary Luke Tobin asserts that "the function of faith is to proclaim the coming rule of God" (1981, p. 119).

   As we Christians struggle with the meaning of the reign and realm of God in the present and future, we are challenged to face political, economic, and social issues—for that is an integral part of our theological task. Whenever we pray, "Thy kingdom come, thy will be done, on earth as it is in heaven," we name the discipleship to which we are called.

   Other faith traditions may use different metaphors to point toward the destination of one's faith journey. Finding ways to communicate about the nature and goal of the journey is an important task for adult religious education. Metaphors like the kingdom of God can provide images that can help us understand and journey toward our destination.

Sabbath. *Sabbath* is another metaphor that needs to be explored in our day. Nourishing the soul requires us to take the sabbath seriously, as does the whole creation. In Hebrew scripture sabbath is both gift and commandment and is set apart; it is holy (Ashbrook, 1989, pp. 2–6). The sabbath year of the earth is foundational and seems to be "the life-sustaining principle of the Creator" (Moltmann, 1989, pp. 63–65). As Heschel observes, "Every seventh day a miracle comes to pass, the resurrection of the soul, of the soul of [humans] and of the soul of all things. A medieval sage declares: The world which was created in six days was a world without a soul. It was on the seventh day that the world was given a soul" (Heschel, 1951, p. 83).

   Both the global environment and human psyches are in need

of recovery. A primary task of nourishing the soul may be to reclaim sabbath or some comparable metaphor that speaks to the deepest yearnings of persons, communities, and the world.

Grace. A metaphor that undergirds Judaism, Christianity, and Islam (Maitland, 1985, p. 51) is *grace.* Christians understand grace as the gift to human beings of unmerited, unconditional love. God's grace is an offer of new life that frees persons from bondage to false gods and fear. "Amazing Grace" sustained slaves in United States history; it also moved them to claim their human freedom.

Grace experienced and internalized offers much to persons and nations that are bound by addictions of all kinds. But gifts have no value (for recipients) until they are received and given a place in their lives. Grace that is received calls forth sacramental living. It provides freedom to live and risk in response to the love of One who is justice-seeking, all-encompassing love.

Smith sees grace as a basic aspect of all religions and discusses it in conjunction with the sovereignty of God (1958, p. 103). Receiving the gift and discovering what it invites or requires recipients to do and be are crucial for faith communities.

Authority. This is the first of six aspects of religion that Huston Smith places at the very heart of all religions that speak to humankind (1958, p. 101). Although *authority* metaphors may grow out of differing stories, all communities of faith need to wrestle with the meaning and nature of authority.

Authority is claimed by some as a way of bolstering the status quo; it is reinterpreted and claimed by others as a metaphor that legitimates empowering all persons by inviting them into an inclusive partnership. In this view authority is seen as "legitimate power only when it opens the way to inclusiveness and wholeness in the household of faith" (Russell, 1987, p. 61). Authority that is used to control and justify dominant viewpoints and cultures and to uphold unjust social orders must be rejected as persons of faith seek to understand and claim God's justice-seeking authority.

Authority is a metaphor that cannot be abandoned, but it must be reenvisioned. It needs to engender personal and social renewal as individuals, communities, and social institutions share authority. Power, like love, must be understood as something to be shared rather than hoarded. Love that is not shared is hedonistic and self-destructive; power that is not shared is demonic.

Christians find that Jesus' life, death, and resurrection embody authentic authority. The church's teaching authority must be grounded in Jesus Christ so that it seeks to include rather than exclude, to invite rather than demand, to act as a model rather than coerce.

The Trinity. The *trinity* invites us to experience the awesome mystery, the saving grace, and the sustaining power of God that empowers us and sends us out to witness and serve in God's name. The holy trinity as metaphor reminds us that God is greater than our understanding and calls us to an awareness both of the transcendence and the immanence of God and of how great the mystery of God is.

The trinity as metaphor may save Christians from focusing too much on any one manifestation of God and believing that God is (only) who we understand God to be. Overemphasis on any one person of the trinity (Father/Mother, Son, Holy Spirit) may lead us to make unbalanced claims. For example, stressing the sovereignty of God the father (and ignoring the maternal side of the creator) led to the doctrine of double predestination; an overemphasis on the son can lead to focusing too much on Jesus the friend and not enough on Jesus the liberator; too much focus on the Spirit can lead to charismatic excesses that ignore the embodied God who acted, as well as acts, in history. The trinity points toward God who creates, embodies self-giving love, dynamically combines "intimacy, urgency and universality," judges, and transforms all creation (see Jenkins, 1990, pp. 42–45). It calls us to honor the mystery of God even as we explore the myriad ways God chooses to reveal God's self to us.

Story for Our Day

For persons of faith, theology is grounded in Story—the narrative accounts of events, passed on from generation to generation, of God's call and promise, of God's commission to gather to worship and to go and serve the world. It is embodied Story and must be embodied in us here and now if it is to be living Story. Story grows out of individual and communal reflection on lived experiences and is a way we have of discerning meaning and responding to mystery.

"God's salvation can no longer be explained in terms of a history moving forward along a straight line. . . . God moves in all directions: God moves forward, no doubt, but also sideways and even backwards. Perhaps God zigzags too. It does not seem God's interest to create neat and tidy landscapes in certain selected places. God goes anywhere a redeeming presence is called for—in Asia, in Africa, as well as in [the Middle East] and in the West. . . . Only God has the original picture. The task of theology is to identify and pick up the pieces that seem to belong to the picture. It is up to God to make use of them in the best way" (Song, 1987, pp. 16-18).

Theology, like liturgy, is the work of the people; it does not require any special knowledge before one can begin the task. All that is necessary is an openness to God's Spirit as one walks with others—in faith, like Abraham—seeking to understand what is and what can be. The experiences (all of them—the good and bad, the joyful and painful, the meaningful and seemingly absurd) and questions of everyone must be brought to the task. The scriptures of the faith community can be shared by those who know the Stories so that they work together to discern what they mean. People can describe their own stories and try to discover connections with those of others who share the journey, as well as ties with the Stories of human beings who have gone before.

Doing theology is the task of every person who seeks to engage in nourishing souls. It means engaging in a process that is authentic because it grows out of each one's experiencing, reflecting, waiting in silence, praying, and acting in faith. It is the work of naming and examining and critiquing and remaking and claiming metaphors that can be revealing to us as we share our stories and seek to relate to the living God by becoming faithful disciples in the world. At the same time it is a task that asks us to be open to the experiences and languages and stories of others who are engaged in the same undertaking. When their language, metaphors, or stories sound strange (or even wrong) to our ears, we may need to work harder at seeing through their eyes.

For Christians the test is the fruits of the Spirit, that is, "love, joy, peace, patience, kindness, goodness, faithfulness, humility, and self-control" (Gal. 5:22; also see Luke 6:43). Justice and love are to be embodied. We must never forget that there were many in Jesus' day who harshly judged the workers who entered the vineyard late in the day and the owner who paid them a generous wage (Matt. 20:1-16), the woman who bathed Jesus' feet with oil and wiped them with her hair (Luke 7:36-50), the tax collectors and sinners with whom Jesus ate (Matt. 9:9-13), and the children whom the disciples wanted to send away (Luke 18:15-17).

Some of the religious people of Jesus' day often failed to understand who God is and what God was calling them to do and be. Those today who are sure they understand the answers to these questions—and who therefore fail to be open to the stories of others and the possibility of new truths—may miss the word of God through prophets and through those outside our own cultures whom God may choose to use to bring words of chastisement or hope.

Hope for the Journey

That some persons are clinging desperately to old ways of knowing and acting seems undeniable. That others are throwing the old ways to the wind and seeking or floundering in other ways and places is also clear. This was true in Jesus' day, and it is true in our own. In science, politics, economics, and religion, paradigms are shifting.

Perhaps a useful metaphor to help us understand where we stand today is that of the old and new wineskins. Jesus said, "Neither is new wine put in old wineskins; otherwise, the skins burst, and the wine is spilled, and the skins are destroyed; but new wine is put into fresh wineskins, and so both are preserved" (Matt. 9:17; also see Job 32:19). Matthew Fox points out that "a wineskin in Jesus' culture was the container on which one's life depended for surviving the long, hot journey through the desert. If the wineskin sprang a leak, it was a life and death matter. The wineskin was portable and supple. A fermenting process went on inside subjecting it to considerable stress. A dried-up wineskin was a dangerous companion for the journey" (1988, p. 82).

There is much "ferment" in our world today. Some will start

out with old wine in old wineskins, and they will complete the journey; the old wineskins will be sufficient. But for many they will no longer do. Some persons will refuse to take the wine on the journey because all they have is old wineskins. They hope to find sources of water for their journey, but they run the risk of dehydration and death. Others pour new wine into old wineskins and head into the desert. It is unlikely, however, that the old wineskins will be able to withstand the hardships to be faced, and they too risk death.

In reflecting on her faith journey, Nelle Morton says, "I came to know home was not a place. Home is a movement, a quality of relationship, a state where people seek to be 'their own', and increasingly responsible for the world" (Russell, 1987, p. 67). Sculpting meaning can be soul nourishing for people of faith. It is an invitation to make this journey of faith our home.

Persons of faith are not alone on their journeys. Jews claim the promise that is revealed in the mighty acts of God in history as revealed in the written and oral Law and the prophets. Christians claim to share with Jews the way of Abraham and Sarah, of Moses and Miriam, of David and the prophets; Christians encounter Peter and John, Mary Magdalene and Martha, Paul and Lydia, the children and the lepers, the tax collectors and sinners, and all who claim the name of Jesus, the Christ, on their journey. Christians and Jews assert that their God is the source of "living water" so that they need not cling to old wineskins or fear the fermenting of new wine.

Those of other faiths also have disciples and prophets who guide them on their journeys. God invites all people to join in loving, serving, and praying for the world.

PART TWO

Fostering Adult Learning in Communities of Faith

Part Two examines avenues for understanding adult learners; it explores differing goals and processes that underlie a variety of approaches to adult religious education. Chapter Three explores human development and the ways people know and learn. Chapter Four considers four metaphors that help us understand different approaches to the task: schooling, faith community, pilgrimage, and new earth. It suggests insights and tools for embarking on faith journeys. Each metaphor explores part of the puzzle that must be solved, as people of differing faiths attempt to create their own paths for individual and corporate faith journeys. Chapters Five and Six offer a framework for teaching and learning in Christian communities that is rooted in the gospel accounts of Jesus feeding the five thousand.

THREE

Knowing and Learning
Throughout Adulthood

What I want to escape from
Is myself, is the past.
But what a coward I am,
To talk of escaping!
And what a hypocrite!
A few minutes ago I was pleading with Michael
Not to try to escape from his own past failures:
I said I knew from experience.
Do I understand the meaning
Of the lesson I would teach?
Come, I'll start to learn again.
                    —*Lord Claverton in Eliot, 1959, pp. 96–97*

A flowing stream is a metaphor for human growth and development. Like a stream, persons find themselves in a complicated, ongoing process; there are no simple cause and effect relationships to
be easily grasped or controlled.

Are there boundaries? Yes. Do people, like streams, sometimes go outside those boundaries? Yes. Are people, like streams,
engaged synergistically with their environments so that each affects
and is affected by all they encounter? Yes. Are they sometimes restricted in their ability to be free? Yes. Do they ever break out from
behind their barriers? Yes. Are they integrally connected to others?

Yes. Do context and environment play significant roles in who they become? Yes. Can any theory or model encompass and explain every question? No. Does that mean that our theories and models are futile and not helpful? No.

Human Development and the Sculpting of Meaning

Humans are wonderfully complex, alive, changing beings who are able to feel, think, will, relate, communicate, care, create, and change. We can learn. Human development is "influenced by symbols created in social interaction" and cannot be understood apart from issues of socialization and the roles of others (Moore, 1983, pp. 96–97). It evolves out of complex, interactive experiences with others and our total environment that we organize in ways that make sense based on our own past and present. Our further development is then influenced by the meanings that we embody. Adult development is most helpfully understood if we avoid making value judgments and take into account those changes that are undesired and devalued by society as well as those judged to be valuable and proper. We must recognize that "developmental changes are sequential in the sense that earlier characteristics help shape subsequent characteristics," but the study of adult development needs to be viewed as descriptive and neither deterministic nor prescriptive (see Knox, 1977, pp. 9–13).

The fashioning of meaning and human development cannot be easily separated, for they are related symbiotically. Both are complex and holistic. They incorporate feelings, thoughts, imagination, and our will and are affected by our biological, psychological, and social selves in the context of our families, communities, and worlds. They are both our own doing and not our own doing. For persons of faith, nourishing the soul must be seen as integrally related to human development as well.

Moore describes the intersection as a big and awesome place where all that is—past, present, and future—meets. Then she says, "This is where religious education must begin, right in the middle, at the intersection. Religious education must begin where person meets person, where person faces future, where person probes past, where person confronts contemporary issues. Persons stand in relationship to God and in relation to the world of past, present, and future. To begin education anywhere other than the middle of these relationships is to split off some segment of life and artificially treat it in isolation from every other part" (Moore, 1983, pp. 110-111).

Viewing religious education as a way of knowing and soul nourishing that takes human development seriously and focuses on the intersections of life as the context for teaching and learning assumes that persons can be actively engaged in their own present and future. At the same time religious education must recognize that human development and teaching/learning can never be individualistic—we are integrally bound to the whole creation in the web of life. The pebbles we drop in the lake affect those we know and those we do not know; we are affected by the pebbles of others even though we may find ourselves on shores far from and unknown by them. The case of the Pueblo Indian who killed the deer (see Chapter Two) illustrates this kind of interconnectedness.

For Christians and Jews, "'*knowing*' always means *know who,* and *know how,* as well as *know that*" (Sawicki, 1990, p. 52). Heschel describes this way of knowing in his account of the way Hasidic Jews learn to read and know the Torah and Talmud:

> Torah study is a way of coming into the presence of God, the Baal Shem taught. A man learning Torah could feel like a son who receives a letter from his father and is most anxious to know what he has to say to him. The letter is precious to him upon every re-reading, as if his father stood there beside him. Persuaded that one should be capable of learning more from people than from books, the Baal Shem sought to add a personality dimension to the study of the Talmud, a great part of whose contents consists of views of sages cited by name. He urged students to seek communion with the sages as well as comprehension of their ideas. Thus, it was maintained that, while learning "Abbaye said" or "Rava said" one should see Abbaye and Rava (as well as understand their utterance). One had to live with them, to enter their minds and souls, not just to grasp their thoughts [1973, pp. 63–64].

Being and acting are the result of this kind of embodied knowing. Who we are and the commitments we make and act on

are the fruits of our knowing. Who we become (our human development) is born of committed knowing.

It becomes clear that *memory* (who? what?) is different from
analysis (how? why?). *Evaluation* requires both memory and analysis and is the process of making comparisons and value judgments.
Reflective, evaluative knowing aids persons in their faith journey
as they seek to make meaning of death and life and to act on what
they come to know.

Building belief systems incorporates all levels of cognitive
knowing that Benjamin Bloom (1956) categorizes as "knowledge,
comprehension, application, analysis, synthesis, evaluation" (Little, 1983). Affective knowing draws on the emotions and includes
"receiving, responding, valuing, organization, characterization by a
value or value complex" (Little, 1983), according to David Krathwohl and associates (1964). The *knowing* that is required of persons
of faith includes both cognitive and affective domains. Finally, people embody their faith beliefs and values, thus involving an act of
will as they carry through on that which they cherish (Little, 1983,
pp. 35–37).

Integration (see Lang, 1983, pp. 82–108) is a key to both our
development and learning processes. Persons at the intersection
who find connections between their past lives and future hopes,
their present experiences, those of others, the faith stories and traditions of their community of faith, and the needs of others and the
world—and are able to integrate them—find life-directing meaning
and purpose that sustain them on their journeys. The ability to
integrate is generally a long and slow process. But once achieved,
it helps to ground the lives of persons of faith. From that time their
life journey involves them in a process of continual reappropriation
of the "story-myths and symbols of [their] faith" as that faith grows
and matures (Lang, 1983, p. 105).

Community provides another key to understanding human
development, the fashioning of meaning, and the nourishing of the
soul. For Christians, *ecclesia*—the body of Christ—affirms the reality of the corporate, interdependent aspect of being truly human
(Johnson, 1990, p. 136).

Developmental Theory

James Fowler suggests that contemporary adult development theorists are able to do for us what storytellers and mythmakers once did for those in primitive and classical cultures. They "name and map our experiences of personal change" in ways that can help us understand that we are not alone and that what might appear to us to be "dis-ease" may really be "a developmental transition" that helps us discover "where we are on the human life course" (Fowler, 1984, pp. 15–16).

There is much to commend the literature of the developmental theorists to us (see Fowler, 1982, and Elias, 1986; see also Glass, 1979, for a brief summary of developmental theories as they relate to ministry with adults and Moseley, 1990, p. 146, for a helpful critique of human development in light of "kenotic [self-emptying] theological anthropology anchored in the suffering of Christ"). Freud, Jung, Havighurst, Erikson, Levinson, Sheehy, Neugarten, Vaillant, Gould, and Gilligan are generally described as writing from a psychosocial developmental perspective. They are concerned with self-image, roles, and relationships as they affect and are affected by moving through the life span. Life phases (seasons or stages) and developmental tasks are viewed as describing common experiences or periods. Kant, Hegel, Dewey, Piaget, Kohlberg, Fowler, and Kegan take a constructive developmental approach that focuses on epistemological questions and examines *how* people know and value rather than *what* they know or do. The patterns and processes human beings use to organize what they know and value are the primary concern of these constructive developmentalists.

I acknowledge important insights from the constructive developmentalists. Fowler and others are asking important questions—questions concerning *how* we discern meaning and develop are basic and need to be explored. His insight that we can be misled if we focus on content rather than process when we study faith development is, I think, extremely important. Yet both process and content are crucial and need to be examined together, as well as in isolation. I believe we must question any system that proposes a dominant paradigm positing only one path (universal, sequential, hierarchical) as Fowler's does, beginning with primal faith and culminating in universalizing faith (1981).

The psychosocial developmentalists offer insights that aid teachers to understand adults and plan ways to engage them in the teaching-learning process. Religious educators can benefit from giving careful attention to their work.

Nevertheless, psychological theories that do not take into account paradox and the imagination cannot provide the *primary* foundation for adult religious education. Rather, we must incorporate what we can from the developmentalists even as we affirm the "imaginative capacities of persons to maintain the inevitable paradoxes of constancy and change, attachment and loss, borne throughout the life history" (Moseley, 1990, p. 161); these capacities provide both energy and insight for those who attempt to sculpt meaning and nourish the soul. For Christians the paradox of "the God-man who died on a cross as a common criminal" and at the same time "has enough staying power to effect the religious transformation of persons and the world" grows out of their faith story and provides a grounding for understanding adult Christian religious education (Moseley, 1990, pp. 158–161).

Story is basic. Developmental theories are attempts to move from metaphorical story language toward conceptual language; this is necessary. But if the theoretical *replaces* the story, rather than growing out of it and then providing clues for those who remain in the story to reflect on, theoretical concepts can become a prison.

Human transformation is a process that seems to "transcend the stages" at times and that "may leap ahead by passing stages and establish an imaginative basis for development that incorporates but is not restricted to the so-called normal sequence[s]" (Loder, 1989, p. 129). Transformation is both work and gift. It cannot be understood without allowing for mystery even as we seek to understand the processes that foster it.

As Moran suggests (1983, p. 24), it is time to recognize that understanding human development is a complex and interdisciplinary task that requires insights and methodologies from many disciplines and that allows for mystery and the activity of the Holy Spirit in the lives of persons, communities, and the universe. One cannot understand human development in isolation.

For persons of faith, it may be more helpful to speak of "deepening our character" rather than "developing the ego through invariant stages." For Christians human development works in tandem with spiritual formation, which involves "a lifelong dynamic of centering, decentering, and recentering ourselves in Christ" as we seek to share in and work toward the reign and realm of God (Johnson, 1990, p. 135). The process of centering, decentering, and recentering is one that may describe Jewish faith development as well. It is an ongoing process as we live and move through life's intersections.

In the difficult places where we may find ourselves, we still need people who will say to us, "Let me tell you a story." We need to tell our stories and hear others' and those of our faith communities that have to do with where we are. We need to wrestle and resist, to cling and venture out, to risk and be loved. Story, ritual, and community can never be replaced by stages as the primary way of understanding ourselves.

Journeying Through Adulthood

> Developmental insights in dialogue with depth psychologies suggest that the young adult dream may reemerge in later adulthood to renew (or block) the power of the adult life. Particularly in mid-life and perhaps again at sixty (or whenever the essential forms of a person's life come under review), the vision that has oriented the set of the adult soul is reawakened for testing and recomposing, and depending upon its adequacy to the conditions of ongoing experience, it may nourish a renewal of energy, vision, and commitment, thus retaining and enlarging its regenerative strength [Parks, 1986, p. 98].

Developmental theories offer us a number of different ways to examine what it means to move through adulthood; they provide a variety of perspectives that may help us better understand the needs of young, middle-aged, and older adults. Erikson's stages (1980), Levinson's seasons (1978), Kegan's upward-spiraling helix (1982), and Perry's journey (1968) all offer models for understanding how adults move across the life span. Alan Knox (1977, Chapter 2) makes clear the powerful role that context plays in human development; it must always be considered as we attempt to understand the questions and the potential that persons bring to their journey. Parks rightly observes that "faith as a patterning, connective, relational activity is embodied, not in the individual alone, but in the social fabric of life" (1986, p. 61).

The broad overview that we will provide of adulthood suggests that we cannot draw clear lines as we seek to describe the life continuum. Chronological age, life circumstances, health, personality, and goals are all variables that affect where we are and how we choose to journey through life.

Stories of pilgrimage are found in Eastern religious traditions—Confucian, Hindu, and Buddhist—as well as in Western traditions. The image for Hindus is a journey from "apprentice (the dependent one), to householder (the responsible one), to seeker of spiritual truth (the wise one)" (Parks, 1986, p. 71). Certainly, Jewish and Christian core stories, as well as their central rituals, reflect journeying in faith. Let us now consider some young, middle-aged, and older adults as they journey through adulthood.

Young Adults. The following passage from Jeremiah describes the first part of the journey:

> Now the word of the Lord came to me saying, "Before I formed you in the womb I knew you, and before you were born I consecrated you; I appointed you a prophet to the nations." Then I said, "Ah, Lord God! Truly I do not know how to speak, for I am only a boy." But the Lord said to me, "Do not say, 'I am only a boy'; for you shall go to all to whom I send you, and you shall speak whatever I command you. Do not be afraid of them, for I am with you to deliver you, says the Lord" [Jer. 1:4–8].

Parks's definitive work on young adults offers a model that describes the movement from "authority-bound forms of meaning-making anchored in conventional assumed community through the wilderness of counterdependence and unqualified relativism to a committed, inner-dependent mode of composing meaning, affirmed by a self-selected class or group." This movement can lead later in life to a "paradoxical convictional commitment" that is interdependent and frees a person to internalize the scriptural description of the church as "many members, one body" (1986, p. 70).

The faith journeys of young adults are characterized by "ambivalence, wariness, exploration, and tentativeness" (Parks, 1986, p. 82). Issues and choices relating to career, friendship and intimacy, family, and life-style are often stressful and may have long-term consequences.

One twenty-two-year-old, who recently graduated from college, got married, and accepted a $31,000-a-year job with good prospects for advancement, told his grandparents, "I thought I would have some money when I got this job, but it is always gone when we have paid the rent, made our car payments, and bought groceries." For some young adults career questions evolve into questions of call and vocation. "I can't bear to think of spending my whole life doing this," one young woman lamented. "Surely there must be something more to life!" Another twenty-two-year-old friend just left for Guatemala, where he will spend the next two years as a Peace Corps volunteer, working with farmers and peasants to improve agricultural practices and rural development. Each of these young adults is struggling to make sense and to become the person they dream of becoming. For those who choose to journey toward and in faith, the task becomes one of nourishing the soul—or "composing . . . the heart's resting place" (Parks, 1986, p. 21).

Because context is so important, we must not move beyond young adulthood before we acknowledge that the needs and gifts of high school dropouts, those who enter the work force or marry immediately after high school graduation, college students (the most accessible young adult audience and therefore the one most described in human development literature), young working professionals (single and married), those in the military, those in the Peace Corps or other volunteer service agencies, upwardly mobile professionals, double-income couples with no children, and young families of varying educational and economic levels each have their own issues and concerns. But they all need a place for their heart to rest. Faith communities are challenged to address the needs of these different groups of young adults—individually or ecumenically (see Merriam and Ferro, 1986, pp. 74–80, for help with program planning and development).

Mentoring by more mature Christians (older and wiser persons of faith) who are open and accepting, skilled at listening and asking probing questions, secure in who they are so that they are comfortable in the presence of conflict and differences of all kinds, and willing to share themselves and their own journeys is a valuable gift that faith communities can offer to young adults (see Parks, 1986, pp. 89–106; Daloz, 1986, pp. 229–235).

It is a judgment on communities of faith when the primary option for young adults who want to socialize is bars. It is crucial in our day to provide a safe and hospitable space where young adults who are willing to share their journeys with other young adults with similar needs can find a home. Offering a place and a convenient time that invites young adults to be together and to share their deepest doubts, joys, gifts, fears, and dreams becomes a primary way for faith communities to respond meaningfully to young adults who are seeking to walk in faith. In most Christian communities I know, that time is *not* before worship on Sunday morning, and the place may or may not be the church building. Relating to young adults requires listening to their needs and giving them the resources to address them as the young people are accepted as full and contributing members of their faith communities.

Middle-Aged Adults. Carl Jung reflects on the journey of midlife:

> Thoroughly unprepared we take this step into the afternoon of life . . . [on] the false presupposition that our truths and ideals will serve us as hitherto. But we cannot live the afternoon of life according to the programme of life's morning—for what . . . in the morning was true will at evening have become a lie [1933, pp. 124–125].

Our son Peter came home from second grade one day (almost twenty years ago) and announced at the supper table, "I know what middle age is!" "What?" I asked. "Thirty!" he announced with the certainty of a seven-year-old. "Oh, Peter," I said. "What does that make Daddy?" "Three years past middle age," was his quick reply. It is hard to pin down what the middle is when the end is uncertain and our culture influences us to avoid thinking about it.

Nevertheless, the middle years are those when people experience times of great change, when "the gains latent in these traumas are largely undervalued," and when many in our day "have overdone self-denial [and] have probably cared more faithfully for others than for themselves" (Maitland, 1985, p. 4). It has traditionally been those decades when men are established in their careers and women are beginning to have more time to pursue their own interests as their children make fewer demands.

What I see for people who are in midlife in the last decade of the twentieth century is a collage so complicated that it defies description. Some who had prestigious and high-paying jobs are now unemployed or underemployed—many through no fault of their own. Some men who feel their experience entitles them to that coveted promotion are being passed over for women or minorities or younger men with highly valued degrees and little experience. Many people face loss of a job due to foreign competition in the marketplace or to obsolete factories that failed to reinvest profits in order to remain competitive.

Spouses who have supported one another in professional growth and development may find themselves in situations where one must sacrifice his or her own career goals if the other is to be able to advance. Commuter marriages become more common every day. Some men find themselves in a situation where the rules have been changed, and they are struggling with what it means to follow their wives and to accept whatever employment they are able to find in a given locale. Women (and men) suddenly find themselves with the responsibilities of being single parents just at the time when social services are becoming less available. Couples who breathe a grateful sigh when the last (these days, not always the youngest) child leaves home discover that they may face on the average more years caring for their aging parents than they have already invested in caring for their children.

As we move through midlife, bodies neither look like nor perform as they once did. There is less energy to meet ever-increasing demands. Health problems require attention and, if ignored, often have life-threatening consequences.

Of course there are those in midlife who are in perfect health, have satisfying careers, enjoy their independence and freedom as single adults or have loving relationships with their spouses and children, are able to engage in enjoyable leisure activities, and find satisfaction in volunteer work. Educational or economic level is not a predictor of satisfaction or success in life. Chronological age is less significant at this stage than are issues relating to "body, career and family" (Neugarten, 1968, p. 94).

Midlife is the time when people review their self-image and may be able to recognize God's invitation "to move beyond preoccupation with self-image to the search for self-knowledge" (Maitland, 1985, p. 5). If questions of vocation (Why am I here? What am I to do with my life?) did not surface in young adulthood, they are apt to do so now. A religious understanding of vocation incorporates "the response a person makes with his or her total self to the address of God and to the calling to partnership" (Fowler, 1984, p. 95).

For most, midlife is a time for purification and deepening of vocation as people seek to clarify what it means to live faithfully as partners with others and the Transcendent. It is often a time of unaccountable restlessness as persons look honestly at their dreams and at the realities of their situations. It can be a period when people who have developed a deepening sense of their own vocation can serve as mentors to young adults who are exploring what vocation may mean in their lives (Fowler, 1984, pp. 138-147).

Mentoring can be a source of growth for both persons. Mentors "offer new cognitive maps, suggest new conceptual language, and serve as mirrors to help protégés see their actions from alternate viewpoints. . . . They are concerned to help people imagine alternatives, question givens, and analyze underlying assumptions. These activities may be unsettling, painful, and anxiety-producing for all concerned, but we persist in them because we believe that out of such experiences come self-insight and more satisfactory lives" (Brookfield, 1987, p. 113).

Midlife is a time when many are engaged in significant giving of self—at work, in their family of choice, to their parents or siblings, and in the religious and other volunteer organizations to which they belong. Middle-aged adults tend to take responsibility for their own learning, much of which is self-designed and performed independently. When it occurs in a more formal setting, these adults want their life experience to be honored: they want to participate in the planning and evaluating of the groups to which they belong, and they want to deal with issues that speak to their real-life issues and concerns (see Tough, 1979).

In an adult Sunday school class I once attended, we studied the lectionary readings and how they relate to our lives. I was among the oldest members in this class; most of the others were in their late thirties and had small children. People in this class expressed a deep need to "be fed" and often referred to tremendous work pressures and the effort involved in getting the family to church for an 8:30 worship service each Sunday. They expected to gain some hope and energy to get through the next week from their learning and worship experiences. Thankfully, simple answers will not do for these people, who recognize that we must wrestle with issues and not accept anything that masquerades as the simple truth. Midlife adults involve themselves and their children in outreach ministries of the church and invest themselves in seeking to be faithful disciples and responsible citizens. (See Slater, 1989, for a case study that can help adults in communities of faith explore the tensions between citizenship and discipleship.)

Faith communities have a responsibility to listen carefully and to join in working with these adults. They must be responsive to the needs of middle-aged adults and help them find *meaningful* approaches to living their discipleship through worship, study, fellowship, and service without loading them down with institutional maintenance tasks; these can lead to the conclusion that the church or synagogue is just one more demand on already stressful lives. Nor can they handle a steady dose of "how terrible the world situation is." They already know that. Instead, these adults need to discover concrete ways in which they can do something to make the world better.

Middle-aged adults have arrived at a place where they can reflect on the intertwining of three strands of meaning: "(1) the dynamism and direction of their personal life narratives, (2) the web of social interchanges in time that constitute their evolving life structures, and (3) the perspectives on the Divine praxis and purpose offered in the core story of the [faith community]" (Fowler, 1984, p. 137). The drama that emerges has to do with vocation, with faith, with discipleship, and with citizenship. It can provide a sense of rootedness and a community of faith in which persons live and move and have their being.

Older Adults. As the following poem attests, acting and reflecting continue till the end of the journey (Snyder, 1981, pp. 84–85).

> I am Awesome Mystery
>   which I will not profane or trivialize
> Nor is anyone else
>   to profane or trivialize.
> Still to be Spirit!
>   though dimly, and at times murky
> Still to be lived moments
>   which light up with significances!
>   even though I am in process of disappearing.
> Still to be a meaningful story
>   since soon that will be all.
> I have a story
>   and I have a song
> And the song will be sung
>   till my day is done

As human beings age, questions of generativity and stagnation, integrity and despair need to be resolved (Erikson, 1980). The need to review one's life and to answer again the question "Who am I?" requires our attention. We probably first posed this question to ourselves at age two or three; we struggled with it in adolescence and again in young adulthood. It seems to be one that follows us throughout our lives. In older adulthood individuals may have the maturity and the perspective to resolve the question in ways that bring peace and free them to live authentically as persons of faith.

At this period of life, chronological age becomes less and less helpful as a developmental guide to persons' abilities and needs. Issues like health and circumstances, as well as personality and outlook on life, become even more important during the last third of the life span. I accept Neugarten's claim that we can predict how people will age if we know their personality traits in middle age and how they cope with change (see Vogel, 1984, p. 12).

Older adults bring many qualities to their communities of faith. The Search Institute research on Protestant denominations in the United States (including Christian Church [Disciples of Christ], Evangelical Lutheran Church in America, Presbyterian Church in the USA, Southern Baptist Convention, United Church of Christ, and the United Methodist Church) reports that older adults (age 60 or more) are more likely to have "integrated faith," which is understood as having both more "vertical faith" (a deep, personal relationship with a loving God) and "horizontal faith" (translation of this personal affirmation into acts of love, mercy, and justice) than younger adults (Benson and Eklin, 1990).

As we age, the reality dawns that those things we have been taught to value by the secular culture (youth, beauty, consumerism, individualism, hedonism, looking out for ourselves) and the addictions to which we may have succumbed (work, shopping, drugs and alcohol, gambling) do not lead to the meaning and purpose for which we long. At an address to the Religious Education Association in 1960, Paula Gonzales observed that our addictive society has led us to a point where we suffer from "malnutrition of the Spirit."

Older adults must struggle to make meaning of death and life as they experience an increasing number of losses. Actually, this reality may enable them to offer life experiences and wisdom to help younger people solve the crises that all humans and the whole planet face. As Maitland points out, older adults may be better able to recognize the illusory nature of much in our society and to set aside some of the social conventions that block many from seeing clearly (1991, p. 122).

The Story and vision of faith communities need to intersect with the experiences of individuals. Both individuals and the faith community must have opportunities to discern the judgment and the hope that the Creator God offers to those who have ears to hear and eyes to see. This hearing and seeing can help people grow toward the justice-seeking, agape-filled rule and reign of God. And this process can happen best in open, accepting environments; people must be invited to speak and hear the truth as they struggle and live with unanswerable questions. The last third of the life span can be a time to risk accepting persons who see and hear differently and to be willing to consider a multitude of responses to the issues at hand.

I believe that older adults should be the *story bearers*, as they are given encouragement and opportunities to share their faith stories. If we do not grasp this opportunity, these stories—and those of that generation's parents and grandparents—will be lost from the community memory (see Benson and Eklin, 1990, p. 48).

The population of the United States, as well as that of many churches and synagogues, is aging. The number of persons sixty-five and over, as well as their proportion of the population, continues to increase. There are even more dramatic increases in the number of people aged eighty-five and over. Predictions are that in the year 2000 persons sixty-five and over will be 13 percent of the United States population and that by the year 2030 the percentage will be 21.2 percent (based on U.S. census data and compiled by the American Association of Retired Persons and the Administration on Aging, U.S. Department of Health and Human Services). The implications for health care, housing, and social services are staggering and must not be ignored by persons of faith who are committed to quality of life for both the young and old in our societies.

A word needs to be said about the frail old, whose needs are great and whose energy and resources are minimal. Faith communities must reach out to this growing number of elderly. We must listen to their questions and their pain, offer a comforting touch, and provide sacraments and rituals that offer "food for weary, hungry travelers."

We must recognize that there are many ways of engaging in educational ministry. When we envision the faith community as the primary locus and strategy for education, it has much to offer to the frail old. Additionally, faith communities must work with and within governmental and private institutions to ensure that our common view of the intrinsic worth of every human being (and of the entire creation) is embodied in social programs that do not leave the most vulnerable (poor, young, and old) alone, in pain, and at great risk.

Scanning Adulthood. These glimpses into young, middle, and old age suggest that there are many paths from which to choose; there are also many different modes of travel. Often, traditional patterns of living and working no longer seem viable. Old answers do not seem to fit the new questions that life thrusts upon us.

What we need is a way of learning to frame and respond to new questions. Persons of faith can assert the freedom to do that as they open themselves to seeing and hearing differently.

New Questions

> Be patient towards all that is unsolved in your heart and try to love the questions themselves like locked rooms. . . . Do not now seek the answers that cannot be given you because you would not be able to live them. And the point is, to live everything. Live the questions now. Perhaps you will then gradually, without noticing it, live along some distant day into the answer [Rilke, 1934, p. 33].

It is undeniably true that we human beings often act out of assumed truths (stereotypes) and that what we have been taught reflects someone else's assumptions and ways of making sense of images, stories, traditions, and concepts from the past; generally, the dominating cultures provide us with the lenses through which we view the world. Our questions prescribe and limit the answers that are possible; many who have been outside or on the fringes of the tradition-forming and controlling power centers of their faith communities and their culture are finding their own voices and beginning to insist on rephrasing and asking their own questions. Women, blacks, Asians, and Christians in places like Central and South America, Asia, and Africa are discovering new power for love and justice, confrontation and care, as they ask different questions. As M. E. Moore points out, "The very phrasing of the new questions challenges dichotomies, such as those between dominant and submissive, logical and intuitive, cognitive and affective, bold and gentle" (1990, p. 71). The answers to these reframed questions are moving persons and communities to debate the validity of the most basic assumptions, and out of this questioning, people are experiencing the Spirit of God afresh. Let me illustrate.

Often when we think of Mary Magdalene, we picture her as a fallen women, a "prototype of sin" (Moore, 1990, pp. 70-71). I asked a group of seminary students what ideas Mary Magdalene brought to mind and their first response was "lust." The second response was "fallen woman." These views are not supported by the gospels. A brief summary of the references to her in the gospels follows:

- One who accompanied Jesus and the twelve and from whom Jesus had cast out seven demons (Luke: 8:1-3)
- One who followed Jesus from Galilee and provided for him during the last week of his life and then stood by him as he died, "looking on from a distance" (Matt. 27:55-56; Mark 15:40)
- One who stood by the tomb as Joseph of Arimathea laid Jesus' body in the tomb (Matt. 27:61; Mark 15:47)
- One who stood near the cross with Jesus' mother and John as Jesus was being crucified (John 19:25)
- One who was among the first who went to the tomb after the sabbath and was the first to hear (from the angel) that Jesus was raised (Matt. 28:1-2; Mark 16:1; Luke 24:10)
- The one Jesus first appeared to who rushed to tell the mourning disciples but "they would not believe it" (Mark 16:9-11)
- The one whose entire conversation with the Risen Lord in the garden is recorded by John (John 20:11-18)

Surely, if we were able to read all of these references to Mary Magdalene with no knowledge of the tradition and teachings of the church, we would conclude that here was an amazing woman who was one of Jesus' closest and most faithful followers—a woman who traveled with Jesus and the disciples, one who cared for his needs and was steadfast in difficult times, the one to whom Jesus first appeared after the resurrection, and one who shared her experiences with others in the community and demonstrated a deep faith and believing spirit when she met her resurrected Lord.

Old questions and traditional answers that were accepted unquestioningly as authoritative led my students to their mistaken view of Mary Magdalene. Now is a time when some traditional ways of viewing faith, family, and work are being called into question or no longer work. This reexamination offers opportunities for going to the roots of one's faith and values and reframing the questions.

We can no longer deny that we have read and heard selectively for centuries—in patriarchal, hierarchical ways. We are much more familiar with male images of God in the Bible than with the female images. Both are there. Yet we rarely refer to God as a mother eagle who tends her young (Deut. 32:11-12; Exod. 19:4); "a woman in labor" (Isa. 42:14); the one who carried Israel in her womb and nurtured her from birth through old age (Isa. 46:3-4); or a woman seeking her lost coin (Luke 15:8-10).

Julian of Norwich depicts the maternal side of God as "enveloping, embracing, welcoming, inclusive, cosmic, and expansive." Meister Eckhart proclaims that all of creation "is bathed in God, is enveloped by God, who is round-about us all, enveloping us" (Fox, 1983, p. 91).

The notion that "doubt precedes belief [and] separation leads to connection" has been called into question, for example, as women recognize that for them, "confirmation and community are prerequisites rather than consequences of development" (Belenky, Clinchy, Goldberger, and Tarule, 1986, p. 194). Both theological content and educational method must be reassessed. The methods of critiquing and reconstructing faith require people to be willing to see self, God, and world in new ways. Old stories must be read with new eyes and reinterpreted as those who have been on the outside or on the fringe learn to value who they are, to trust their own experiences as useful, and to find their own voices to speak truth as they discern it.

"In making nurturance, caring, concern, and connection goals of education," we must also foster a union between these reproductive (feminine) processes and those generally associated with the productive (masculine) dimension of life—"rationality and autonomy" (Martin, 1985, p. 197). A new understanding of wholeness that recognizes that many of what we have traditionally understood to be feminine or masculine characteristics needs to be valued, developed, and affirmed in every man and woman.

As the world is threatened with chaos by the reframing of questions and the restructuring of world views, there is a danger that those who ask new questions will be co-opted and given a corner of the action in the old world. But it is not possible to leave the world as it has been if we commit ourselves to ask these new questions. By daring to live the questions now, we embark on a journey that may direct us toward answers that require new ways of being and relating. These have the potential for leading us toward the realization of God's reign and realm.

Dialogue in Teaching and Learning

> Truth is before us as mystery, reality, and the wonder of that which is transcendent, which stands as reference, corrective, and source of power to those who seek to be conformed unto it. . . . Belief in truth, though we do not possess it, constrains us, and propels us to continue seeking honestly, faithfully [Little, 1983, p. 90].

Upon completing a Bible study session, the adult students were given an opportunity to reflect on the experience. One man said, "She didn't really teach us. It was more like she invited us to reflect and share." For many, *teaching* means lecturing; *learning* means being told. In this section we will explore what it means to use dialogue in teaching and learning—so that all are learners, and each has something to share that can contribute to the growth of all.

In *To Teach as Jesus Did* (1973), the United States' Catholic bishops assert, "Those who teach in the name of the Church do not simply instruct adults, but also learn from them; they will only be heard by adults if they listen to them." This recognition that adult learners now insist on participating in the dialogue is an important first step.

Paulo Freire suggests a context for using dialogue as a means of searching after truth when he says that "dialogue cannot exist . . . in the absence of a profound love for the world and for [human beings]." It requires "humility [because] the naming of the world, through which [we] constantly re-create the world, cannot be an act of arrogance." It requires "an intense faith in [humankind], faith in [their] power to make and remake, to create and re-create, faith in their vocation to be fully human" and hope, which moves us to both "fight" and "wait." Finally, dialogue requires "critical thinking . . . which discerns an indivisible solidarity between the world and [human beings] and admits of no dichotomy between them—

thinking which perceives reality as process, as transformation" (1970, pp. 77–81).

To foster critical thinking in others requires us to name our assumptions (biases) at the outset, as well as when we become aware of them along the way, and to encourage others to do the same. By declaring our "values, assumptions, and biases from the beginning" and then engaging in the process of making "a critical examination of their validity," we establish trust among those who seek truth together and begin the dialogue (Brookfield, 1987, p. 66). Once people engage in the process of critical thinking, their world view is expanded, and they are able to consider a variety of options for making sense of experience and discerning truth.

Learning in this fashion requires a radical departure from a transmissive approach. It views the "mastery of information and memorization" as "servants of critical awareness and perceived relevance" rather than as an end. It includes everyone in the process of naming the goals and working out the methodologies that will engage participants in learning what they want or know they need (Wren, 1977, pp. 27–29). "Authentic education is not carried on by 'A' *for* 'B' or by 'A' *about* 'B', but rather by 'A' *with* 'B', mediated by the world—a world which impresses and challenges both parties" (Freire, 1970, p. 82).

Knowledge is understood as "designative rather than prescriptive"; this idea frees groups to be able to work toward consensus. The goal is "not to establish cause-effect relationships but to increase insight and understanding through symbolic interaction" (Mezirow, 1985, p. 20).

Learning by dialogue begins with what people know, rather than what they do not know. It encourages participants to draw on their past experiences and their future hopes as they attempt to share their own insights and questions and listen to the insights and questions of others. There must be a willingness to confront conflict and to engage in assessing every idea in order to move beyond any one person's ideas toward collective insight. This kind of knowledge does not consist of right or wrong answers. Individual contributions are offered, considered, and set aside, or they are affirmed and corrected as the process continues. Finally, the group arrives at consensus, the highest truth that the community is capable of discerning.

It must be noted that consensus is not a majority decision; nor does it necessarily represent complete agreement by all of the participants. Rather, consensus occurs when everyone (1) acknowledges that they have been heard, (2) believes that their opinions have been seriously considered by the group, and (3) is willing to accept and act on the group's emerging understanding. It is possible, then, for individuals to agree to a consensus that was not their preferred outcome. But until all are able to say yes to all three conditions, the work toward consensus must continue.

This idea of group consensus is not within the experience of many in our win/lose culture. The League of Women Voters and Quaker meetings provide us with models of how this kind of learning can enhance the quality of community and of group decision making.

My daughter, who attended Earlham College, explained her experiences in a community that operates on a consensus model like this. When people go to a meeting, they take their ideas along, but they know that the decision that will be made will be better than any one person's idea. People offer ideas for consideration without fear of personal attack. It sometimes takes a long time to make a decision, but the community just keeps working at it until everyone can live with the outcome. Sometimes a person says, "I must stand outside the consensus, but I know I have been heard and I am willing to live with the community's decision."

Learning by means of dialogue is cooperative rather than competitive; open rather than predetermined. It can provide a context for learning that fosters "critical reflectivity, which is what makes [personal and communal] meaning transformations possible" (Mezirow, 1985, p. 25).

Principles for Teaching and Learning

As people begin teaching in communities of faith, they must first examine their assumptions about God, faith, the nature of the faith community, about the nature of commitment and discipleship and about adult learners. Then they must actively incorporate their understanding of these issues into their teaching.

On the one hand, if a teacher understands Christian religious education to be "a political activity with pilgrims in time that deliberately and intentionally attends with them to the activity of God in our present, to the Story of the Christian faith community, and to the Vision of God's kingdom, the seeds of which are already among us" (Groome, 1980, p. 25), this understanding establishes parameters regarding the nature of both content and process. On the other hand, if one understands the goal to be seeking to lead people to a personal conversion experience and to accept Jesus Christ as their Lord and Savior, the parameters for planning and teaching would be less likely to include issues relating to political activity and social transformation.

Whatever one's understanding, it seems clear that people who choose to teach in faith communities must be aware of and take into account the symbiotic relationships among individual learners; the group; the images, stories, and concepts of the faith tradition; and the culture(s) where people live and work.

Adults are most ready to learn when their current way of being and doing appears unable to solve some problem. When people encounter cognitive dissonance, they enter a "teachable moment" (Brookfield, 1986, p. 31).

When we use dialogue for teaching and learning, we must be sensitive to the gifts and needs of each learner. Daloz (1986) suggests that mentors (mentoring is an important role of the teacher) need to provide "support, challenge, and vision." *Support* involves listening, confirming, offering appropriate structure, being clear about expectations, becoming an advocate, and sharing ourselves by being willing to be vulnerable and honestly sharing some of our own journey (pp. 215–223). *Challenge* may involve creating cognitive dissonance, setting tasks, requiring accountability, focusing on dichotomies, suggesting possible hypotheses, maintaining high standards, and pushing learners to reframe their questions (pp. 223–229). *Vision* grows out of the supporting, challenging relationship between teacher and learners. It recognizes that teachers are models. Providing vision may include walking side by side with the learner, offering alternative maps, introducing new language, and holding up a mirror so that learners can glimpse the now and move into the future (pp. 229–235).

Using dialogue means that teachers do not bring ready-made answers to learners. "The teacher, like any lover, must be capable of having a lover's quarrel with the subject, stretching and testing the loved one and the relationship. In this way students are invited into the negation as well as affirmation, into argument as well as assent, within the secure context of friendship and hospitality" (Palmer, 1983, p. 104). The teacher's openness and willingness to struggle can evoke a similar response from learners.

Inviting learners to tell their own stories and frame their own questions is a crucial part of the dialogue. In other words, listening—between the lines as well as to the words actually spoken—is one of the most important teaching tasks. Teachers who truly listen, and who do not misuse what has been shared, are well on the road to creating trust. Trust is a prerequisite to being able to challenge learners by raising questions and introducing cognitive dissonance.

Accepting the role of challenger means that teachers have to be willing to risk introducing conflict. At this point in the teaching-learning process, I sometimes find comfort in reminding myself that I am called to be faithful, not to be popular and my students' favorite person. Introducing conflict that may cause pain can be painful for the teacher, too, but it is sometimes inevitable.

Providing vision does not mean telling learners what is wrong with their answers or giving them *our* answers. It means being called to "emphasize positive movement, underline it, restate it, praise it" (Daloz, 1986, p. 127). It means using stories from their lives, the culture, and the faith community that may offer new ways of envisioning where the group wants to journey. It means showing how integration can take place while encouraging learners to picture a future from our understanding of God's grace and call (Moore, 1983, pp. 116–117).

Learning that truly engages learners at every level, that involves the whole person, and that manifests itself in commitment and action is the most personally fulfilling and socially beneficial (Rogers, 1969, pp. 162–163).

Methods of Using Dialogue for Teaching and Learning

Methods put "questions in motion." They are the vehicle that "activates our learning" and "invites students to try on, explore, and test the meaning and implication" of the life issues being explored (Foster, 1986, pp. 72–73). Methods propel us on our journey in faith. They are the ways we have of structuring our search for answers to the questions that challenge and frustrate, push and pull, us along the way.

Sometimes when we think about ways to teach, we place too much emphasis on techniques and not enough on how people integrate their own life experiences with the images, stories, rituals, and concepts of a given discipline. Method in religious education has to do with providing learners with structures and tools for exploring the meaning of life and death, faith and commitment, in ways that open them (1) to their own stories; (2) to the stories, rituals, values, and beliefs of their faith community; (3) to God's Spirit, who guides and empowers persons and communities; (4) to the reality of the reign and realm of God, which is both now and in the future; and (5) to God's call to each one of us to committed living in the world, while taking seriously the larger cultural contexts in which people live.

Methods are not gimmicks to make teaching easy or to keep learners happy. They are a means to critical reflection and creative imagination, which help "illuminate meanings from the Scriptures for our life and time," find ways of linking "the holy with the everyday" existence of our lives, and enable us to embody "those meanings for actions of justice in the world" (Seymour, O'Gorman, and Foster, 1984, p. 149). We must heed the warning to be found in Brookfield's observation that "when technique is worshipped to the exclusion of the human or social purposes it is meant to serve, then it is easy for us to become dazzled by the convolutions of the latest shaman of procedure and by the pronouncement of those who flaunt commonsense ideas regarding teaching and learning under the guise of presenting a revolutionary paradigm of practice" (1986, p. 289).

Too often, using dialogue in teaching and learning has been

assumed to involve having a good discussion. Leading discussion
has been taken to mean teaching with little or no preparation. Both
assumptions are false and give education and teaching bad names.
Teaching through questioning is vitally important and requires
careful planning. Teachers must be attentive to the context and to
the experiences and questions of the learners before they articulate
questions. Learning will be enhanced by questions that move from
the more factual toward the evaluative and through levels of awareness toward committed living (see Harris, 1987, pp. 174-175).

As we have seen, methods must be provided that challenge
us to respond in affective and creative ways, as well as in cognitive
and analytical ways. Because human beings bring very different
learning styles and a myriad of different gifts to the teaching and
learning community, those who teach must provide opportunities
for persons to enrich the group with their unique qualities and
artistry and insights.

Harris offers an invitation for teachers who desire to practice
imaginative teaching and learning to create their own models and
methods. She suggests that we devise our own ways of engaging
students by following five criteria or paths: (1) *taking care*, which
requires being open to the Spirit and creating an environment for
learning that honors the value and integrity of all; (2) *taking steps*,
which means participating in the dance of "contemplation, engagement, form-giving, emergence, and release"; (3) *taking form*, which
has to do with embodying the subject matter so that persons can
encounter it in holistic ways and begin to interact with it; (4) *taking
time*, because birthing is a slow process that cannot be hurried and
revelation is a gift that one must patiently await; and (5) *taking
risks*, because teachers who dare to be vulnerable and to risk loving
in the face of resistance—and who seek to be there for those who are
in the process of discovering who and whose they are—will discover
that teaching is a calling from God (Harris, 1987, pp. 158-181).

Three Groups of Adults Who Learned

Creative teaching and learning in communities of faith means recognizing the complexities involved in understanding how adults
grow and develop; it entails accepting that we and all persons need

to examine our assumptions and become open to new ways of framing questions and imagining possibilities; it means searching for approaches to listening and speaking that can open doors for both teachers and learners. Here are accounts of three varied groups of adults who taught and learned as they sought to journey together in faith.

Knowing and Learning at Trinity Church. A group of adults meet about once a month at Trinity Church on Saturday from 8:00–10:00 A.M. to talk about issues of faith and life as they have been framed by the author of a book that the group has chosen to read. Saturday mornings are not my favorite time for religious education, but I decided to read Stephen Jay Gould's *Wonderful Life* and to attend one of these sessions. When the alarm went off on that cold February Saturday morning, I resisted the temptation to stay in bed and drove to the church.

There I found thirteen others who had also read the book and braved the bad weather. The group ranged in age from those in their early thirties to persons well into their seventies and included eleven men and two women. All were professionals—scientists, lawyers, CEOs, professors. We spent two hours raising questions, sharing insights, and exploring issues of life and death, of faith and hope. Notes I jotted down from that lively discussion include:

> "We're on several collision courses for the future of the world."
> "What is the key to the Christian faith?"
> "Helping persons be able to make sense—to synthesize."
> "Not asking people to affirm what they do not believe."
> "To help us struggle with faith issues metaphorically."
> "Doing this [kind of learning] and worshiping in community is what it's all about."

As we were leaving, one retired man said to me, "You know, this is the first church I've attended where you don't have to check your mind and your sense of humor at the door!"

Knowing and Learning at a Shelter for Battered Women. A friend of mine is a pastor in a city near a large metropolitan area. She serves on the board of a shelter for victims of domestic violence and was asked to lead a Bible study at the shelter. She was familiar with Ernesto Cardenal's *The Gospel in Solentiname* (1976-1982), four volumes of biblical interpretation that report the discussions of people in base communities who had gathered to hear the reading of the gospel text (usually by a boy or girl, as many of the adults could not read), to share in the mass, and then to talk about what the Bible said to them. These commentaries were created from a dialogue born of biblical text, the experiences of people who are poor and victims of injustice, and the power of the Holy Spirit.

The approach described in Cardenal's book seemed appropriate to engage these victims of violence in scripture study. The method recognizes the valuable life experience of all participants, and it asserts that formal education is not a prerequisite for having insight into God's Word. Questions are used to encourage participants to enter into the scripture passage and to attempt to discover what it means to them.

"Initially, I went to *lead* Bible study," my friend said. "Now, I go to *join* Bible study." She agreed to the inclusion of this portion of one evening's dialogue, which followed breaking of bread together and then hearing the Word. (The names have been changed, and my friend chose to remain anonymous to protect the women in her group.)

The scripture is read: [Jesus is speaking] "Or what woman having ten silver coins, if she loses one of them, does not light a lamp, sweep the house, and search carefully until she finds it? When she has found it, she calls together her friends and neighbors, saying, 'Rejoice with me, for I have found the coin that I had lost'. Just so, I tell you, there is joy in the presence of the angels of God over one sinner who repents" (Luke 15:8-10).

Gloria: Jesus is saying, when you've lost your sense of worth, you better do some cleaning out!

Mary: Ya—weren't these coins like all this woman had? It would be like losing my welfare check one month—I'd be desperate!

Sis: Boy, you know—when I start looking for something I've lost, I find a lot of other things I've forgotten I had under all the clutter—

all the garbage—things which I value but have forgotten. That is part of the joy of finding, I think. We find more than we seek.

Mary: Ya, and these welfare checks, and ADC [Aid to Dependent Children], they're garbage, and we start looking for them like they are silver.

Jeanne: Jesus says light those lamps and *see* what you've really lost, sweep those corners of your life and quit sweeping trouble under the rug.

Sis: And when we find what we are really worth—not what my man swore I was—"Good for nothing!"—then God will rejoice because believing I am good for nothing is a sin. Jesus didn't die for "good for nothing." Jesus decided I was "worth dying for."

Jeanne: Jesus, I'm sweeping as fast as I can.

Knowing and Learning in the Inquirer's Class at Calvary Church.
When we moved to Iowa after graduate school and began teaching at a small liberal arts college, we joined the Inquirer's Sunday school class. "There is only one requirement," we were told, "you have to have an open mind!" The class was made up of young adults—married and single. Sometimes, only one spouse came to this class while the other went to a different one.

Leadership was shared. We studied books on suffering and evil, world religions, Genesis, Mark's gospel, environmental issues, peace, faith, and politics; we even worked our way through 720 pages of Hans Küng's *On Being a Christian*. We had some lively discussions and had to struggle to resolve hurt feelings from time to time. We became a real community that cared about one another and the world.

During the twenty years we belonged to that class, one of our members was diagnosed with multiple sclerosis. We shared the struggles of a young family with four sons, as the wife and mother valiantly fought and died from breast cancer and a brain tumor. One of our number ran for the United States Congress. We discussed the pains and joys of raising kids, the vocational struggles that face persons as they move from young adulthood into middle age, and our hopes for and frustrations with the institutional church. We talked about the things that mattered to us.

We have been gone from that community for six years now and recently went back for a visit. At a party in our honor, we talked about our kids, war and peace, the environment, our church, the economy, the college where we had taught and some of them still teach, travel, our vocations, faith struggles, retirement, and our grandchildren. Friends from graduate-school days were there—new members of the Inquirer's class, as it carries on its traditions and serves as both refuge and launching pad for a group of adults who want to be faithful disciples of Jesus Christ. It is adult religious education. It is the church as it grows and learns, is faithful and unfaithful, is forgiven and empowered by God.

FOUR

Four Ways
of Experiencing
Adult
Religious Education

To be open-minded does not mean to be willing to make compromises with the truth. But truth is very elusive. . . . We are more likely to catch glimpses of truth when we allow what we think and believe to be tested. Truth does not seem to flourish when imprisoned in rigid dogmatic statements or in an infallible teaching authority. It seems to prefer the company of persons from all walks of life. Let us be clear, then, that it is not our business to protect the truth. Rather it is our business to serve the truth wherever and whenever it is found.

—*Song, 1987, p. 15*

Religious education is not something that can occur or even be examined in a vacuum. It is not something that takes place only in classrooms or at set times. It is not primarily for children. It *is* a lifelong process of learning and claiming the metaphors and stories that identify who and whose we are; of developing skills in reading and internalizing scripture that can provide maps for living; of discerning what we need to take (and what we must discard) for our journeys; of learning to trust others and being willing to share both our joys and sorrows along the way; of knowing where we can find food and water that satisfies our needs; and of preparing and sharing in celebrative banquets to which *all* creation is invited.

Readers are invited to reflect on their own understanding of religious education. What are the goals? How might you define or describe it to others? The following paragraphs are my attempt to do that. Use them as dialogue starters. Are there insights that help you? What would you say differently? What have I left out? Educating in faith happens in many different ways and places. The ideas here are meant to be food for thought, not the only or last word.

Religious education invites purposeful engagement with the faith community's Story, our own stories, and those of all persons and communities as we are able to come to know them. It is engagement that involves reflecting on our own and our community's actions in the world, in light of their metaphors, stories, models, and concepts of our faith, in order to discover who we are and what God would have us do. Goals of religious education may be understood as (1) calling individuals to listen and share life experiences and stories as they intersect with one's faith story; (2) building community through worship, study, witness, and service; (3) clarifying problems that block justice and then working to bring about a more just and caring world.

Religious education should be perceived as an active process over the entire life span through which the faith community seeks to call persons into ever-deepening relationships with God and each other, and the whole of creation so that they might join together in worshiping in spirit and truth, learning that leads to committed living, being instruments of the God who requires justice and loving mercy, and sharing in the fellowship of their community of faith.

Christian Religious Education

As persons (and communities) find new life in Christ, Christian religious education calls them to commit themselves to "living in the risen Lord," which means being called to embody justice-seeking love that is not bound by the fear of death; to nurture "spiritual growth in the gospel" through disciplined prayer, meditation, worship, and service; to participate in "confessional conversation within cultural pluralism," which means we must know both the language behind the wall and the language(s) at the wall; and to be willing to accept the "holy insecurity within tenuous communities" that will not allow us to fall victim to easy answers or closed systems; to work for the "liberation from poverty and oppressiveness" of all God's children; and to risk "living toward the grace-filled future that is given by the Creator" (see Seymour and Miller, 1990, pp. 239–258).

Christians throughout history and those in our own century have understood the task of religious education in a variety of ways. Metaphors have blossomed into models for guiding faith communities in their educational task (see, for example, Seymour and Miller, 1982, and Little, 1983). Metaphors offer us ways of moving toward new possibilities (Palmer, 1983, p. 61); metaphors with "staying power" develop into models. Models are less fluid than metaphors and provide "sufficient stability and scope so as to present a pattern for relatively comprehensive and coherent explanation" (McFague, 1987, p. 34).

It may help us to examine four metaphors—(1) *schooling*, (2) *pilgrimage*, (3) *household of faith*, and (4) *new earth*. All four should be seen as metaphors of both place and process. These metaphors underlie the approaches of Christian religious educators to educational ministry. Out of these metaphors, models of Christian religious education have developed, as people have sought to find ways of involving adults in naming what it means to be a disciple of Jesus Christ and a member of the body of Christ.

Teaching and learning in faith communities rarely, if ever, reflect only one model. There is overlap and interplay among the models themselves. What is being suggested here is that metaphors can support models that begin with different basic assumptions and that illuminate certain ways of knowing and acting. Coming to see what our basic approach is to teaching and learning in communities of faith can aid us in being both conscious and purposeful about ways we plan and teach. It can also help us discover the strengths and weaknesses of our own approach so that we can enrich it with other models.

Schooling as Metaphor. "Now every year his parents went to Jerusalem for the festival of the Passover. And when [Jesus] was twelve years old, they went up as usual for the festival. . . . they found him in the temple, sitting among the teachers, listening to them and asking them questions. And all who heard him were amazed at his understanding and his answers" (Luke 2:41-47).

Teaching and learning have been a way of transmitting faith for centuries. Schooling is a part of our experience that can provide a metaphor for understanding what it means to teach and learn faith.

In my interviews with several older people, we explored their attitudes about school and religion; they indicated that negative experiences in school still have a profound effect on them and color their decisions about whether or not to participate in classes offered by their churches. Some persons have had negative experiences in Sunday school that affect their attitude toward joining in anything that resembles school. People's past experiences with classes, teachers, and classmates and their attitudes toward learning do affect decisions about participation in adult religious education, as well as the expectations they bring to teaching and learning in the church (Vogel, 1981). Interestingly, some drop out of religious education classes when the format changes from lecturing to a more interactive process because they expect a more traditional method. Their past experience affects whether they want the current one to be the same or different.

Our images of ourselves as gifted or mediocre or poor learners have been developed in large measure by our school experiences. How we view teachers, classmates, curricula, and class is baggage we bring to teaching and learning settings in communities of faith. These attitudes and experiences provide a context for understanding "the schooling model of education in the [faith community]" (see Miller, 1987, pp. 300-301). Jesus was in school when he was twelve years old and remained at the temple "sitting among the teachers, listening to them and asking them questions" (Luke 2:46). Synagogues still function as settings for adult religious education. Luther's catechism classes were a primary vehicle for teaching the faith. Sunday schools were vitally important instruments of adult education (as well as for the education of children and youth) in churches as they developed across this land. Sunday schools have survived and are growing in many places in spite of numerous attempts to move beyond or eliminate them. Other long-term classes for adults (for example, *Disciple, Kerygma,* and *Bethel* series) offered in church settings are being well attended.

What images does schooling create for you? For me, it suggests classrooms; teachers and students; a topic or subject to be explored; some structure, generally provided by the teacher; the use of a variety of resources, including but not limited to books; and a variety of activities (including field trips) that involve give-and-take among students and teachers as together they try to master content and solve problems.

As education is a purposeful activity, schooling seems to be one appropriate metaphor for stimulating our thinking about teaching and learning about religion in structured settings where there are clear content and behavioral goals. Because it evokes so many feelings and creates certain expectations, the schooling model has been getting bad press of late. Somehow, religious-instruction and information-processing models (which are often equated with a schooling model, much to the chagrin of those who work with them) have also come under attack. Yet I believe that the schooling model continues to be a valuable one and that schooling is a primary metaphor from which the religious-instruction and information-processing models of religious education have come.

The religious-instruction model, as it has been developed by Lee, is grounded in the social sciences and draws heavily on the discipline of education. Little's information-processing model is grounded in theology. Both emphasize the importance of structuring the learning environment and designing teaching and learning plans so that students will come to understand and believe the traditions and tenets of the faith and live in obedience to its teachings. When one examines these models, it becomes clear that they are directed at goals, the roles of teachers and learners, content, strategies for helping students engage the content, settings, curriculum, and methods of evaluation.

Little points out that attention must be paid to moving between generalizations and particularities so that "propositions or concepts can always be documented by concrete data" (1983, p. 40). Dykstra describes the role teachers may embody when he says "the teacher actually hopes for certain changes in another person's life (in knowledge, thought processes, insights, perceptions, feeling and/or action), and acts in ways that will facilitate those changes" (1981, pp. 124–125). These models focus most heavily on the cognitive; they take seriously the need to transmit the scripture, traditions, doctrines, and life-styles of the church.

It must be noted that Lee (1971, 1973, 1985), the chief proponent of the religious-instruction model, and Little (1982) object to equating schooling with a religious-instruction model. One reason Lee objects to linking schooling to the religious-instruction model is that the model encompasses religious teaching "wherever, whenever, and however this mode of teaching is enacted" (1985, p. 746). So long as we are clear that schooling as metaphor brings images and expectations relating to both process and place, his objection seems less necessary. Schooling does connote teaching for most persons, and it suggests ways that we can design settings, curricula, and processes that will engage persons in learning about faith.

Interestingly, society's understanding of what it means to be in school is changing dramatically in our day. More and more adults are participating in universities without walls. An eighth-grade friend just spent four days with his teachers and classmates in Washington, D.C. My seminary class is going to Japan in January to study and travel with Christian educators there. I have students who spend all night working in a shelter for the homeless as a part of their school work. All of these experiences might be understood as legitimate activities within a religious-instruction model because they are part of a plan for learning through experiencing and then reflecting on what one has learned. Schooling as metaphor for this approach to adult religious education may become even more apt in the future as schools claim "whenever and wherever and however" as legitimate parts of their domain.

There are several precautions that must be taken when persons and communities choose to engage in religious education using models that reflect schooling as metaphor. We must avoid the trap of assuming that *learning about* is the same as *encountering* the living God. We must find ways to involve and receive contributions from those adults who may be stronger in creative and affective domains than in critical, analytical ways of knowing.

Among the strengths that models related to schooling can contribute to the religious education endeavor are (1) making accessible and passing on the church's traditions (persons, events, stories, rituals, values, and creeds); (2) developing a shared memory and a common vocabulary that are absolutely essential if people are to know who they are and be bonded to a faith community; (3) learning the language of faith for conversations behind the wall as well as the language(s) for dialogue at the wall; (4) offering a structured and formal way of encountering content and process that fosters appropriation; and (5) helping human beings develop the skill to reflect critically on matters of religion and faith in order to understand, decide, and believe.

Pilgrimage as Metaphor. "My faith journey has not been a continuous one or a steady climb up the ladder of 'faith development.' It has been desultory and meandering. There have been sickening reversals and absurd contradictions. There have been times in my life when I have lived more in the past than in the present, when memories of events gone by have seemed more vivid than what was happening under my nose. There have been detours and dead ends. Sometimes my journey takes me past the same landmarks several different times" (Cox, 1983, p. 23).

Life is a journey from birth to death. It is both unique to each individual and shared by all. There are many signposts along the way that would have us believe that this or that route is the most attractive or direct. But not all signposts are equally trustworthy. We are offered guarantees and enticements and promises of free rides. There are roads that should be marked "dead end" but are not. And there are rocky paths that look threatening but may lead through the valley of the shadow of death to a table where our cup is filled to overflowing (Ps. 23). Guilt and shame, hedonism, and self-giving love each offer different maps to guide us along life's journey. The signs we trust, the invitations we reject and those we accept, the friends we choose to accompany us on the journey, and the maps we select all play a part in the direction and course of our pilgrimage.

Pilgrimage as metaphor opens us up to the realization that all our lives are in motion. Whether we meander without direction or set out with a sense of purpose, there is nothing static about human existence. Teachers may be seen as guides and as gatekeepers for the journey. When we teachers view ourselves as guides who are willing to share our knowledge of the territory with others, we find joy in having companions for our journeys and are able to teach rather than to tell (Daloz, 1986, p. 243). The gatekeeping role reminds us that it is sometimes necessary to "stand at the boundary of the old and the new worlds" to caution and to challenge (p. 96). The teacher as midwife is an image that suggests that we are not to anesthetize; rather, we are called to "assist in the emergence of consciousness" and to foster and encourage persons to do their own thinking, to discover and develop their own insights and to act on what they discover (Belenky, Clinchy, Goldberger, and Tarule, 1986, pp. 217–219).

There is always the danger that those on a journey will forget from where they came. Harris reminds us that "our history of forgetting (pogroms, persecutions, perjuries) as well as of remembering will have to be addressed" (1989b, p. 68). Although we are always free to change directions and to travel toward radically different destinations, those who forget where they have been (both personally and as a community of faith) are very likely to misread the signs and make poor choices about where they are going.

To risk being guide, gatekeeper, midwife, and companion on the way is a holy task. It is to be vulnerable and to acknowledge that we, too, are on the journey of life and faith and do not have all the answers. But "if teachers [in faith communities] would take off their shoes on each teaching occasion in the conviction they are on holy ground, they could envision this truth more easily" (Harris, 1989b, p. 117). Teaching and learning are what pilgrims do together on the journey. Our joy is doubled and our grief is diminished because we do not have to carry either alone.

Pilgrimage is a key image for Thomas Groome's shared-praxis approach to Christian religious education. To understand ourselves as "pilgrims in time" who are undertaking the work of appropriating our past and setting about purposefully to create our future as we live and struggle together in the present is the task of Christian religious education (1980, p. 261). The Hebrew and Christian scriptures provide us with our vision for the future God intends—the reign and realm of God (see pp. 35-36).

"If we are going to talk the talk, we have to walk the walk," the saying goes. Pilgrimage reminds us that those who would teach faith have to walk with people who travel along many different parts of the road. It calls teachers to know the Stories of the faith so that during the walk they can share stories appropriate to the place and the decisions that must be made.

For example, Exodus took on new meaning for the Jews in Babylon after Jerusalem was destroyed; it assumed new meaning for the slaves in the United States as they struggled for their freedom. The exodus-wilderness experience of the Hebrews carries power for the struggle and assurance of God's gracious love for human beings who are not free and who face their own wilderness experiences. The task of the teacher becomes a sacramental act of embodying and sharing the power of God's mighty acts as they illuminate our everyday experiences with the mystery of the creating, saving, sustaining God.

We need to remember the way Jesus related with those two disciples on the road to Emmaus. Pilgrimage as metaphor has blossomed into models of shared praxis (Groome, 1980) and hermeneutical circles (Brown, 1984). It can help us envision ways that persons of faith can embody revelation and the faith community's message and mission as they seek to understand and to respond in faith.

Clues about settings can be found in biblical stories as well. As we travel together and share around the table, we can be companions to each other. In our day church and synagogue board and committee meetings are appropriate times and places to help persons focus on their task in light of their faith.

Pilgrimage does not lend itself to easy answers or to fixed doctrines. Rather, it pushes us to acknowledge the stresses that people encounter and the different perceptions that they hold and to see both as opportunities for making decisions about next steps, which signs to trust, which maps to carry with us, and who our companions will be on our journeys. Above all, we need to remember that "their story, yours, mine—it's what we all carry with us on this trip we take, and we owe it to each other to respect our stories and learn from them" (Coles, 1989, p. 30).

There are dangers in these models as well. When persons focus on stories and journeys, it is easy to forget that there is one Story of faith in which all our stories should be rooted and in the context of which they need to be understood; it is this Story that calls us to accountability. Whenever we use theology to reflect on experience, we run the risk of being captured by the dominant culture and our own powers to rationalize.

Models reflecting pilgrimage as metaphor offer possibilities to religious education that include (1) focusing our attention on the need to engage in an ongoing process of action and reflection as we seek to make connections between our life experiences and the faith community's Story; (2) emphasizing dialogue that begins with the learners' own stories and affirms that real learning takes place at the intersection of stories and the Story through critical reflection; (3) recognizing persons are more apt to "act their way into belief" than to "believe their way into acting"; and (4) acknowledging that learning must be holistic—cognitive, affective, and volitional—so that one's beliefs, actions, and values grow out of actively holding past, present, and future in creative tension.

Household of Faith as Metaphor. "No one's faith journey begins at birth. It starts eons back with the mothers and fathers of our great-grandmothers and great-grandfathers, and before. Our faith seeps into our corpuscles carried on the songs we hear before we know what their words mean. It enters us with voiceless grimaces, smiles, and distant looks, whispered secrets, tics, smells, stories, all incorporated into our tissue before we are aware of it. It comes to us bound up with caste and class, with color and gender, with language and cuisine. We all meet ourselves, as Sören Kierkegaard once put it, on a ship already launched, a journey already under way" (Cox, 1983, p. 14).

We learn what it means to be a Baker or a Thornburg or a Bliege or a Hernandez or a Lee by growing up in our particular households. There are no classes. There is no stated curriculum. But the message generally comes through loud and clear. Those for whom a household of faith metaphor is primary rely on the lived life of the faith community; they give special attention to its story and liturgical life and to insights from sociology and anthropology as they develop models for engaging in religious education.

God called a people, and ancient Israel was born. The Israelites learned who they were and what it meant to be in a covenant relationship with God by embarking on a journey that led Abraham and Sarah from Haran to Canaan. The journey took Joseph to Egypt, first as a slave betrayed by his brothers, then as a servant, a prisoner, an interpreter of dreams, and finally as the agricultural secretary of Egypt, which enabled him to save his family from the famine in Canaan (Gen. 37-50). The journey required Moses to choose between his royal Egyptian family and God's call to claim his Hebrew birth and lead the Hebrew slaves out of bondage—but the Hebrews whom God liberated lost faith when they perceived that there were giants in the promised land, and so their journey led back to the wilderness, where they wandered for forty years, received the law, and became a people with an identity (Exod. 2 ff.). Human beings become faithful by living in a community of faith and by discovering what it means to claim its stories and values as their own.

Rabbi Neil Gillman says, "I was inhaling Judaism from the cradle on. Soups and candles and boiling cabbage and latkes and gefilte fish, kasha, kreplach, pot roast. . . . [Today's seminarians] are smart, and the intellectual stuff they get easily, but it's hard to get the other; the ritual sensuality of Jewish religious life. The guts of it. How do you teach that?" (Wilkes, 1990, p. 70). Those preparing for ministry today (Protestant, Catholic, and Jewish) may or may not come out of faith communities. But if they do not embody their faith family's stories and rituals and life-styles, how are they to nurture others in the ways of their faith family?

Christians understand the need for this kind of nurturing when they reflect on Paul's assertion in his letter to the church at Ephesus: "So then you are no longer strangers and aliens, but you are citizens with the saints and also members of the household of God, built upon the foundation of the apostles and prophets, with Christ Jesus himself as the cornerstone. In him the whole structure is joined together and grows into a holy temple in the lord; in whom you also are built together spiritually into a dwelling place for God" (Eph. 2:19–22).

Our faith communities provide a "relational context where we are known personally (over time), where we are taken seriously, and where we are invited to submit our images of ourselves and our vocations to trusted others, who are informed by the community's 'script' and core story, for correction and/or confirmation" (Fowler, 1984, p. 126). Persons who learn by participating in a living organism—the household of faith—may become, through its "worshipping, believing, [and] serving" an "incarnational expression . . . [of] the collective life of the people" who faithfully reflect "its own inner depths" (Grierson, 1984, p. 36).

Story and ritual acts are at the heart of models developing out of the household of faith metaphor. Morgan's definition of Christian religious education asserts that it is "the church passing on the tribal lore" and "drawing people into the clan so that they know its way of life and are proud to be part of the clan" (1986, p. 106). "Daddy, tell me a story" is the door to a powerful way of educating in faith. "Mommy, tell me about when . . ." is a teachable moment that gives us the opportunity to tell and retell the stories about who we are and who we can become. It is in the telling and hearing (over and over) of our shared stories that we learn that we belong and that the household of faith as both place and process is our home.

Nelson maintains that "faith is communicated by a community of believers and that the meaning of faith is developed by its members out of their history, by their interaction with each other, and in relationship to the events that take place in their lives" (1976, p. 10). The emphasis here is on interdependence, shared Story, shared liturgy, and a common calling to witness and serve in the world.

Persons learn by living together—worshiping, praying, sitting at table and breaking bread together, sharing one another's burdens, and working. Values and life-styles and beliefs and stories become a part of who each person is because they are a part of the household of faith—it is their family, and they reflect that understanding in every dimension of their living. What happens in community is that "an emotional attachment to the significant others" develops; and without that, "the learning process would be difficult if not impossible" (Berger and Luckmann, 1967, p. 131).

But there is always the danger of idealizing one's household of faith; this does violence to the metaphor. If we truly know the faith story, we will recognize that the people of God in the Hebrew scriptures and the disciples who walked and sat at table with Jesus were not living in ideal communities. There was as much human sin evident in those communities as there is in ours today.

Palmer reminds us, "Community is that place where the person you least want to live with always lives!" (1981, p. 124). Jesus exercised "the discipline of 'staying at the table'" (Raines, 1984, p. 106) when the disciples who had walked to Emmaus failed to recognize him and at the last supper when he knew that the one who would betray him was present. Being part of a household of faith requires us to listen to and accept those who disagree with us and whom we do not like very much.

By claiming to be a part of a faith community, individuals are incorporated into its ethos, which contributes to the development of their self-identity. Socialization is a dynamic, ongoing, lifelong process since both the individuals and the faith community are in the process of growing. Marthaler suggests that socialization can provide a model for Christian catechetics that must ultimately be judged by how adult members of the faith community "understand and carry on the mission of Christ in the world" (1978, p. 90).

One of the dangers of building a model for religious education solely out of the metaphor household of faith is that the model may lack procedures for discerning and holding both persons and the community accountable for "distorted or absolutized" ways of knowing and being faithful to the tradition (Boys, 1989a, p. 137). This can lead to the belief that a particular household embodies the only way of living and being a community of faith. This false image of community can lead to "escapist behavior [that] denies God's call to heterogeneity and the transforming of culture" (Westerhoff, 1985, p. 21); or it can lead to disillusionment with the faith community, which causes persons to leave.

Gifts that models growing out of the household of faith metaphor offer us include (1) learning the stories, ritual acts, values, and life-styles that bond people to the faith community and contribute to their emerging self-identity; (2) recognizing that all that is done in and on behalf of the faith community is the curriculum in the school of faith; (3) fostering opportunities for intergenerational interaction that focus on the communal nature of faith; and (4) emphasizing the centrality of affective learning and bonding in the process of becoming persons of faith within faith communities.

New Earth as Metaphor. Both Hebrew and Christian scriptures offer powerful, poetic images of the new earth. The prophet Isaiah writes:

> For I am about to create new heavens and a new earth;
> the former things shall not be remembered or come to mind.
> But be glad and rejoice forever in what I am creating;
> . . . .
> They shall build houses and inhabit them;
> they shall plant vineyards and eat their fruit.
> They shall not build and another inhabit;
> they shall not plant and another eat;
> for like the days of a tree shall the days of my people be,
> and my chosen shall long enjoy the work of their hands
> [Isa. 65:17-22; also see Rev. 21:1-4].

Participating in creating a new earth (the reign and realm or kingdom of God) requires a renewed faith and engagement in reconstructing society. People of faith are called to join together to study and listen to one another and God's Word, are empowered by God's Spirit, and find a new freedom to live (and if necessary, die) as they invest themselves in working for justice. In more affluent churches, there is the danger that the vision of the Kingdom of God tends to lose its power and be seen as an abstract and nonpolitical or an other-worldly concept. Jung Y. Lee reminds us that "the Kingdom of God that Jesus preached was . . . meant to be a concrete and real world where justice and the love of God would be actualized in real-life situations" (1988, p. 15).

Story is also central to models that evolve out of a new earth metaphor. As the story is told, retold, encountered, owned, and reconstructed, "a new dynamic is generated in the encounter between the tellers and the hearers of that story" (see Brown, 1988, pp. 38-44). Living story is story that speaks to each of us in the time and places where we find ourselves. Story is not something that has to be mastered; rather, it grasps us and will not let us go. We see ourselves and our life situations in it; it identifies our pain and offers us hope. It challenges us to risk becoming involved in living story that can indeed move us and the whole creation toward a new earth.

The Kingdom of God as understood by Korean Christian minjung theology symbolizes that reality where "the history of Christ and the history of the world intersect" and "the painful past is brought to Christ's healing presence" (Koyama, 1988, p. 147). This intersection can be the place where human beings bring who they are and who they hope to be. There, in the presence of past injustices and atrocities that we have committed and that others have committed against us, we are called to repent and mourn. In the presence of Christ's gift of forgiveness and new life, Christians are offered a vocation to become a part of the body of Christ and to become co-creators with God and our sisters and brothers to work toward the coming of the Kingdom of God in its fullness.

This metaphor of a new earth blossoms in Reverend Park Sun-ai's poetic reflection on the agenda facing the women's movement in Asia:

> A stone is thrown
> into a calm lake
> and the stone made waves
> spreading, reaching to the far end
>
> Till the whole lake
> Starts bubbling with life
> Till the whole lake
> makes its own spring
> to keep its own life going
>   23 April 1985 [Russell, 1988, pp. 78–79]

Transformation and liberation models of adult religious education spring up from the new earth metaphor. Although we are all aware of dramatic instances of radical transformation (Paul's conversion on the road to Damascus, for example), transformation is more often a gradual process that may become visible to others first, and only later do we recognize it in ourselves (Daloz, 1986, p. 60). It is a process the requires time, commitment, and hard work.

"It is impossible to think of transformation," says Freire, "without thinking of getting power to transform" (quoted in Evans, Evans, and Kennedy, 1987, p. 226). Models of religious education for transformation and liberation require persons to work to gain and then use political power in ways that combat injustice and create a just society for all persons. But we must avoid being co-opted by existing structures that may be willing to share some power (if we are willing to compromise our goals).

For Christians the power of the cross is "power out of weakness, life out of death, resurrection out of the cross." It is "power from below [that] is mutual and reciprocal enhancement of the community." It may be the church's (and our own) hesitancy to engage in struggles for political power on behalf of justice that leads Freire to urge Christians to "do Easter" or "make Easter" and not to just talk about it (Evans, Evans, and Kennedy, 1987, pp. 272–274). Models so that those of us who must identify more with oppressors than with the oppressed can begin to participate in transformative education must include "encounter with the poor and experiential immersion that challenges [our] assumptions." There must be an "openness to vulnerability" as well as "support and accountability." Vision, critical analysis, and engagement are all necessary. "Symbol, ritual, and liturgy" also play significant roles in the transformative process as persons of faith willingly risk being changed and becoming agents of change who are committed to work toward the coming of the new earth (Evans, Evans, and Kennedy, 1987, p. 274).

Dialogue is a primary tool for transformative education. It requires that all be able to find their voices and to engage in the meeting between persons; it recognizes that each person has much of value to offer. It requires skills in critical thinking and a deep trust in the God who invites all persons to take part in the dialogue and who promises to be present in the struggle for justice (Freire, 1970, pp. 76–81).

There are dangers inherent in this metaphor also. When people forget that the promise of a new earth is a gift, they have a tendency to become consumed with the enormity of the task and to give up. There is the propensity on the part of many well-meaning persons of faith to want *to be* "a voice for the voiceless" rather than to move over, "so that the voiceless can not only have space on the platform but also get control of the mike" (Brown, 1980, p. 58).

Models derived from the new earth metaphor can contribute by (1) recognizing that human worth and a just world are gifts offered to everyone by a loving, justice-seeking God; (2) demanding that religious education cannot be separated from life but must take place at its very center, where history and hope intersect; (3) affirming that what each one brings to the teaching and learning experience is valuable and must be treated with respect; and (4) asserting that encountering the scriptures, talking together, worshiping, and acting in the world must always work together in the wholeness of faithful living.

Metaphors not only undergird models of religious education, but they can also be powerful ways of sharing about faith and hope. The following example, born out of a liberation model of religious education, returns us to metaphorical ways of knowing and acting in faith.

A Reading from the Book of Real Life

Our communities are like a tree. In the ground, invisible to the eyes, are the roots, whose tips are at once the strong and the weak point of the tree. They are its strong point because through these thousands and thousands of tips the tree sucks up the sap of the earth. They are its weak point because the ends of the roots are fragile, so fragile. The least shock damages them, bruises them. Without this permanent fragility in the roots, however, the tree cannot rise up out of the ground healthy and strong, cannot replenish itself and keep on living. This fragility must be maintained, even cultivated, certainly not eliminated! The higher the tree, the deeper and broader the root must be.

This is what gives the tree its strength. Thus strength appears as the culmination of weakness. In other words, what is strong and powerful is human contact, spontaneity, the risk of events, conversation, personal problems, a whirl of friends, informality, disorganization and seeming inconsistency—in the midst of a people who are poor, weak, and suffering, people marginalized and oppressed, people voiceless and voteless, people struggling for survival, people with little instruction or study, people with innumerable problems. This is the weak, ever-renewed root of the strength of our great tree which is grown now: our communities [Carlos Mesters, *Una Iglesia que nace del pueblo*, quoted in Galdamez, 1986, p. 6].

This description moves me because I believe we are all "fragile roots," even though some have more resources and power at their disposal than others. To those of us in more affluent world nations and churches who have been given so much, much will be required. But the task of religious education is to encourage everyone to risk sharing their vulnerability and to acknowledge that they are often overwhelmed by life. It is to offer faith communities useful metaphors and models, though these must remain open to being changed by new situations and possibilities.

FIVE

Creating an Open Environment for Teaching and Learning

All the great religious teachers say with one voice that to meet the living truth, we must let it come to us and speak to us *where we are*. We must be faithful to the text and to ourselves.

—*Morrison, 1986, p. 8*

In Chapters Five and Six, we will look at the story of Jesus feeding the multitude as a way of understanding what it means to serve as a guide and companion for persons who journey in faith. These two chapters create a model for approaching Christian religious education.

A Story About Jesus

It had been hectic for many days—people coming and going, trying to do more than there was time to do. They were all tired—bone-weary. And then the news had reached them. When they heard it, they were stunned!

But those who brought the news vouched for its accuracy. Jesus' cousin John had been beheaded by Herod. Herod had created a dilemma: the only way he could save face was to do as his wife asked and to present her with John's head on a platter.

Jesus, too, was stunned. Why had this happened? What might it mean? He got into a boat to get away, to find a place to try to sort out his feelings and the meaning of it all.

Even when he needed it most, time alone and space to think eluded Jesus. As he got out of the boat, he discovered that many people had followed him by land and were waiting for his word and his healing touch.

Once again, he put aside his own pain and frustration, his own confusion and anger, and responded to their needs. He reached out to them and healed their sick.

"Bone-weary" no longer described how Jesus and his disciples felt. They were exhausted in body, mind, and spirit. As it began to get dark, the disciples looked at their beloved teacher and said, "It is already very late, and this is a lonely place. Send the people away, and let them go to the villages to buy food for themselves."

They were startled when Jesus replied, "They don't have to leave. You yourselves give them something to eat!"

Hurriedly they looked from one to the other; they may have wondered if Jesus had lost his senses. "Do you want us to go and spend two hundred silver coins on bread in order to feed them?" Imagine, two hundred silver coins—it took a farm worker a whole day to earn one silver coin!

But Jesus ignored their startled disbelief and said, "How much bread do you have? Go and see."

Too amazed to do anything else, they did as Jesus asked. Soon they came back and said, "Five loaves and also two fish."

It was spring—almost time for Passover—and the usually barren landscape was invitingly green. Jesus told his disciples to divide the people into groups of fifty and have them sit down on the grass.

Jesus took the five loaves and the two fish, looked up to heaven, and gave thanks to God. He broke the loaves and gave them to his disciples, who distributed the food. Everyone—at least five thousand men, as well as women and children—had all they wanted to eat. Once everyone was full, Jesus told his disciples to gather up everything that had not been eaten; when the disciples finished, they had twelve baskets of food left over (based on the gospel accounts).

The feeding of the five thousand is the only miracle of Jesus found in all four gospels: Mark 6:30-44, Matthew 14:13-21, Luke 9:10-17, and John 6:1-15. Other synoptic accounts that may refer to the same experience are found in Mark 8:1-19 and Matthew 15:29-38. There are, of course, differences in the gospel accounts, which are helpfully compared in *The Anchor Bible* (Brown, 1966, pp. 240-243). Our focus will be on this important *story* of the faith as it provides some important clues for human beings who are seekers of truth. We will focus on how Jesus responded to the pilgrims who followed him to see, to learn, and to find wholeness.

In Touch with the World

The larger context for teaching and learning in faith communities is the world. In all four gospel accounts Jesus' feeding of the multitudes is an activity that grows out of his sensitivity toward tired, hungry people. Beyond that, it is Jesus' actions in the world—his teaching and miracles and healing—that cause the crowds to follow him to a lonely place. It is an awareness of the great need of people in the world that moved Jesus to send out the twelve (Mark 6:6b-13). It is a political act—Herod's beheading of John the Baptist (Matt. 14:1-12)—and the people's rejection of Jesus' authority (John 5:19-47) that leads Jesus to withdraw to a lonely place.

An important principle for teaching and learning is to balance involvement in the world with withdrawal for reflection and renewal. An action-reflection model of teaching and learning (see Little, 1983, pp. 78-85), which attempts to move us from examining to living our beliefs, may remind us of the need for this balance.

Religious education that insulates us from the problems and potential of the global village in which we live does not follow Jesus' example. Christians are called to be in touch with the world. Whenever we insulate ourselves from the greed and misuse of power by individuals and institutions, the pain and death that touches millions—those in our own neighborhoods and in *all* neighborhoods—we are ignoring Jesus' openness to the needs of all people.

When Jesus heard the news that John had been beheaded, he

withdrew—to grieve, to assess, and to gain strength to move out into the world once again to act on his beliefs.

As persons of faith, we are called to be sensitive to the needs of all kinds of people: young and old; black, brown, yellow, red, and white; married and single; well and diseased; uneducated and well-educated; poor and rich; gifted and ordinary; discouraged and exuberant; fun-loving and contrary; immoral and virtuous. Now that is not easily done.

We are all blinded by stereotypes. Stereotypes allow us to bracket certain groups of persons so that we do not have to deal with them. Stereotyping makes our world more manageable. Stereotypes also give us a way of dealing with our fears and anxieties.

What adjectives come to mind when you hear "Americans" or "Russians" or "Indians"; "homosexuals"; "liberals" or "fascists"; "fundamentalists"; "the filthy rich" or "the dregs of society"? We all make assumptions about groups of individuals. We could not function without generalizing. But many assumptions we hold are not based on well-documented data. We may have had a bad experience with a few individuals in a particular group, and so we assume that everyone in that group will be like those we have known. Our knowledge may even be second- or thirdhand.

Being in touch with the world requires us to examine all of our assumptions. Some, we will determine, are appropriate (for example, the idea that low self-esteem often results in antisocial behavior), and others will have to be discarded (Christianity and democracy are synonymous).

Being sensitive to the needs of all persons—especially those who are different from us—is part of what it means to be connected to the world. It means listening to hear and not to refute; it means seeing through the others' eyes rather than only through our own; it means showing empathy and care rather than disdain and judgment.

Being in touch with the world requires us to seek to grow and learn. We need to examine issues from multiple points of view. One way to do this is to read and expose ourselves to viewpoints contrary to our own. We need to develop friends who do not think as we do about every issue.

It is comfortable, in our rapidly changing world, to surround ourselves with people who think and act as we do. Sometimes this practice leads us to believe that all good people must be "like us"— a defense mechanism that quickly causes us to lose touch with the real world. When leaders of the United States can say, "There are no hungry people in America," we become aware of how deluding this approach can be.

Being involved in the world is often disconcerting. It robs us of our pat answers and our familiar remedies. Jesus asked his disciples to look at the problem from a different perspective. They assumed that there were more hungry people than there was food or money to buy food to feed them. Jesus jumped outside the limitations of their assumptions. He changed the question from "Do you want us to go and spend two hundred silver coins on bread?" to "How much bread do you have? Go and see" (Mark 6:37–38).

This more open approach requires us to examine the assumptions we hold and to explore alternative ways of seeing and doing things. In addition to becoming more aware of the parameters that limit us, we need to consider expanding or changing them. We are challenged to reframe the questions. Think, if you will, of times when you have been bound by self-imposed (in reality, perhaps nonexistent) limitations.

An illustration of these self-imposed limitations is found in the following exercise: Without lifting your pen from the paper, connect all nine dots by drawing four straight lines. You may cross another line but do not retrace it.

· · ·

· · ·

· · ·

Were you able to complete this task the first time you tried? (One solution can be found at the end of this chapter.) This exercise illustrates how we are controlled by assumptions that are self-imposed and may be false. By questioning our assumptions and experimenting with different possibilities, we find the answer.

This openness to reframing the problems we confront and examining the parameters that limit our possible responses challenges us to ask hard questions, to consider alternatives beyond the obvious ones. It pushes us to be more expansive and inclusive as we seek to make meaning.

More than a decade ago, Alvin Toffler (1980) described "the third wave," a revolutionary movement that propels humankind beyond the industrial revolution. The movement is, he asserted, the result of deep psychological, economic, and technological forces that foster cultural diversity and challenge old ways of thinking and being.

Robert Theobald (1987) describes our turbulent times and claims that the traditional ways of behaving are no longer valid; we must learn how to work and live in a diverse world—being passionate without being intolerant; living the present moment aware of our past but without the security of old answers. We must be open to the future that we are creating, recognizing that we cannot yet imagine or envision it.

Theobald asserts that, in order to traverse these rapids of change, we need "servant leaders" who accept both their abilities and their limitations. These servant leaders must be open to new truths, compassionate, just, honest, humble, and loving. They must be life-affirming and move toward basic human values that are held by people and cultures around the globe.

Dialogue becomes a primary resource for those who would become servant leaders. Dialogue with persons from differing cultures and faith commitments requires that we know our own behind-the-wall language so that we are clear about what it is that we believe and hope; we must also be fluent in at-the-wall languages so that others will be able to understand what it is we have to contribute and so we will be able to understand the contributions of others. Dialogue causes us to look at people and issues from different angles; it helps us be in touch with the world.

Teaching and learning in a faith community call us to be involved in the world—being connected to all kinds of people and issues. It is being connected with the God of Abraham and Sarah,

Moses and Miriam, David and Michal, Deborah and Samuel, Hosea and Gomer, Jeremiah and Job, Peter and Mary Magdalene, Paul and Lydia, the lepers, and the Samaritan woman at the well. For Christians it is being connected to the Creator God, through Jesus Christ who showed us what it means to be servant of all. Jesus was so much a part of the world that he gave his life to save all creation.

In Touch with God

Where do we turn to find a rudder to steer us through the rapids of change? What do we do when we feel threatened on every side and the world seems to have gone crazy? When we recognize that we live with discontinuity and diversity, in what can we trust?

Jesus knew that everyone requires solitude at times—to get away from the crowds and the demands that are made, in order to be still and know the living God. The need to be alone and to rest is crucial. When we acknowledge our need to be quiet and listen for the Word of God, we are better able to keep on course. Keeping sabbath is one way human beings are able to keep in touch with God.

Jesus and his disciples had to deal with the shocking news of John's beheading and to prepare themselves for the Passover celebration. They needed to reconnect with the story of God's saving activity in the world. They sought time apart.

It is easy for us to be so involved, so hurried, that we do not take time to be quiet and think about who we are and who God would have us become. We can be so overwhelmed by our fears and doubts, our anxiety and preoccupations, that we cut ourselves off from an awareness of God's presence and abiding love.

As we saw in Chapter One, Tad Guzie (1981) makes clear our need to stay in touch with who and whose we are by discerning the way our "raw experience" becomes "lived experience" through naming and reflection; this lived experience—which has not only been experienced but begins to be internalized and related to our past and future—blends into our "story". Then our story must be acknowledged, owned, and celebrated in "festivity." This cycle is one way of describing the process that helps us remain grounded in our faith. We saw this cycle in the account of the two disciples on the road to Emmaus. We can see it, as well, in the story of the feeding of the five thousand.

How often we settle for just existing. We may describe it as "the treadmill of life" or "our humdrum existence." We may feel victimized and out of control. We cannot make meaning of who we are or what we do, so we just continue on the same path.

My fear is that many of the Christians who attend church sporadically have lost, or are in danger of losing, touch with the Gospel Story. They attend because they have always gone, because it is a good thing to do, because they want to raise their children to be good citizens, or because their friends are there. When we talk with them about why we do what we do in worship, it becomes clear that they see little connection between their lives and the worship life of the congregation. We must help persons *make connections between their own life experience, the faith community's Story, and worship.*

One crucial way for Christians to reconnect with the Gospel Story and to make it their own is by *reappropriating the power and meaning of the eucharist* or holy communion. Clearly, the accounts of the feeding of the multitude demonstrate that Jesus saw what he did that day as relating to the people's experiences and expectations of the Passover, in which they lived again the saving act of God in the exodus. (Note the comparisons on the chart found in Brown, 1966, pp. 240–243.) One of the powerful ways Christians have of being in touch with God is in the celebration of the eucharist. Yet many Protestants seem not to have experienced the power that God offers as persons of faith gather around the table to be fed.

The eucharist ought to be a powerful sign-act in worship that helps participants focus on God's mighty acts in Jesus Christ. The eucharist is a wonderful gift—a means of grace. But Christians become unable to appropriate and receive the gift in its fullness when they lose touch with their faith story.

Henri Nouwen spent two extended periods at a Trappist monastery in the Genesee Valley in New York. During a seven-month stay, he disciplined himself to write a simple and honest prayer at the end of each day. Reflect on these lines from one of these prayers: "How often do I sing the psalms but remain deaf! How often do I see the bread and wine yet remain blind!" (1983, p. 43).

How often we see and taste the bread and wine—eating and drinking without recognizing that this is our lifeline, our connection to the ongoing, creative, saving act of God!

The celebration of the Passover was a central experience in Jesus' life. Jesus fed those Passover pilgrims who had followed him to a lonely place. This event seems to provide a link between God's saving gift of manna in the wilderness (see Stegner's chapter, "The Feeding of the Five Thousand," in *Narrative Theology in Early Jewish Christianity*, 1989), God's saving act in the exodus that was celebrated at Passover, and the meaning of Passover that Jesus would fill with new meaning for Christians as he celebrated the last supper with his disciples.

The liturgy of the eucharist rehearses the Christian story (as we see in Chapter One). Those who believe are recipients of God's saving act in Jesus Christ. They are called to be God's children. They are forgiven. They are free to live their lives as faithful servant leaders whose commission is "to do justice, and to love kindness, and to walk humbly with your God" (Mic. 6:8b). (See Brueggemann, Parks, and Groome, 1986, for a brief but powerful explication of how this passage might inform our educational ministry.)

A six-year-old child responded to the question "What did you do in Sunday school today?" like this. "My teacher, we made bread together, and I ate mine already and it was good!" (Dykstra, 1980, p. 901). Dykstra observes that as Christians we "make bread together" whenever we share our stories—Bible stories, stories of people of faith across the centuries and around the world, and our own stories; whenever we give of ourselves in listening, loving, and caring; whenever we worship—singing, praying, hearing, responding.

We receive a wonderful gift whenever we take the bread and cup: Christ's body, broken to give us life; Christ's blood, shed that we might receive the saving, liberating love of God! As Christians we are called to "do this in remembrance. . . ." Remembering the story of God's saving acts from creation to this very day keeps us in touch with God.

This knowledge of God has been described as "an entering into truth, a knowing that we belong to God, a feeling of security, a knowing of our place in God's plan [which] provides incentives to commitment and change" (Gillespie, 1988, p. 48).

Sometimes by being in touch with the world we receive a distorted sense of who God is and what God would have us do. In our time we are becoming aware that our view of God has been distorted by an overemphasis on what Matthew Fox has called "fall-redemption" theology to the exclusion of a "creation-centered" theology.

For example, we have seen suffering as the wages of sin but not as the "birth pangs of the universe." We have focused on "climbing Jacob's ladder" rather than on "dancing Sara's circle" (Fox, 1983; note especially pp. 316–319).

Recognizing biases and distortions is nothing new. It is a natural outcome of persons seeking to walk faithfully with God. It was a process that led some Christians to move from participating in slavery as an accepted part of the created order to joining others in decrying it as incompatible with the reign and realm of God.

Being in touch with God is much more than feeling close to God. In fact, sometimes we may feel that God is far from us or does not hear our prayers; our feelings can deceive us, and we must not allow them to determine our realities. Being in touch with God is knowing—in a holistic, Hebraic sense—that God is, that God loves, that God saves, that God calls us to be faithful disciples, that God judges, that God is the alpha and omega.

Being in touch with God must not be seen as a manipulative tool that we use to control others. The history of the church contains many examples of persons claiming that they were doing God's will while engaging in violent, oppressive, inhumane acts.

When we are truly in touch with God, we experience a deep humility. There must be a commitment to *working to liberate* rather than oppress, *to love* rather than change, *to serve* rather than control. There is a recognition that we do not always have to be right; we can be open to finding truth wherever we are and from every person we meet.

When we know God's presence in our lives, we discover that we are free to look at the problems and evil in our world through new eyes; we are able to respond with hope rather than despair. Because we no longer feel pursued by the needs of the world, we are freed to reach out in love and care.

We are able to join with Nouwen in praying, "O Lord, let

me enter into your presence and there taste the eternal, timeless, everlasting love with which you invite me to let go of my time-bound anxieties, fears, preoccupations, and worries" (1986, p. 85).

Because Jesus was in touch with God, he dared to trust that God does provide. "Taking the five loaves and the two fish, he looked up to heaven, and blessed and broke the loaves, and gave them to his disciples to set before the people; and he divided the two fish among them all" (Mark 6:41).

Being in touch with God means listening, trusting, acting, being; it means *saying yes to God's great gift* and claiming the name and the responsibility that results from our affirmation: "I am a child of God."

Creating a Hospitable Space

In order to care for the hungry crowd, Jesus created a space that changed a crowd into manageable groups of fifty (Luke 9:14). All four gospel accounts record that Jesus instructed all the people to sit down. It is hard to shove and push when one is sitting down. Jesus created a space and an atmosphere for a wonderful picnic supper.

When the crowd (now broken into smaller groups) was ready, Jesus began a ritual act with which the people could identify. Thousands of persons en route to Jerusalem to celebrate the feast of the Jews must have seen and heard with understanding as Jesus took the loaves and fish, gave thanks to God, broke the loaves, and gave them to the disciples, who gave them to the people.

As we engage in teaching and learning, we, too, must actively create a space and prepare people to be touched by the power of God. Henri Nouwen has suggested that hospitality can serve as a model for creative teaching and learning. "Teaching," he writes, "asks first of all the creation of a space where students and teachers can enter into a fearless communication with each other and allow their respective life experiences to be their primary and most valuable source of growth and maturation" (1986, p. 85).

Environments provide *confirmation*, introduce *contradiction*, and offer *continuity* (Kegan, 1982). The environment is much more than the setting where learning occurs. As Daloz suggests,

"We both create and are created by our environment" (1986, p. 192). Environments are places, words, gestures. They exude a life of their own: cold or warm, inviting or threatening, safe or fearful.

Creating a hospitable environment for teaching-learning experiences is a primary task for teachers. It involves being sensitive to both the physical and social environments. The creation of a social environment is the most critical. Nouwen speaks of creating "a free and fearless space" with safe boundaries. It is a space that engenders mutual trust so that teachers and learners together can be present to each other (1986, pp. 84-90).

For too long, the faith communities have been answering questions that people were not asking. We have been teaching *about* God rather than sharing our own experiences with God. We are not called, first of all, to teach for mastery of content. We are called to create a secure and free space where persons gradually learn that it is safe to reveal who they really are. It is an environment in which people can encounter God's Word as it speaks to their own stories and questions and be transformed—they can be made whole as they accept God's gracious love.

Teachers and learners together create a space where each can dare to be vulnerable, where each can look honestly at their own life experiences and seek to make meaning of them all. It needs to be an environment where persons can express anger and doubt without being judged; it needs to be a place where persons can speak without embarrassment about how God has touched their lives.

This hospitable space fosters community. When adults engage in Christian teaching and learning that focuses on what it means to follow Jesus, that community is the church. As the church, we are invited to eat and be filled, to drink and be satisfied. It is at the Lord's table that we are truly fed. So it is that we return to the power and the comfort that is present when we break bread together. It is not an accident that breaking bread was central in both the Emmaus story and the feeding of the five thousand.

The celebration of the eucharist—if it is to be all Jesus showed us it could be—cannot be an isolated event. It grows out of our learning times and our worship times, our fellowship and our service. The eucharist is that moment when we are graced by the power of Jesus' broken body and shed blood. We are graced by the self-giving love of God.

How does one create this kind of hospitable space? It has to do with being authentic, being willing to reveal ourselves in appropriate ways. It is hard to admit—even to ourselves—our imperfections. We want to be admired and respected.

It involves listening and helping the group learn to listen to one another. How much we miss, and how often we misunderstand those who risked sharing and were not heard. It has to do with helping each other dare to hear the questions that grow out of our living and that may be buried deep within our hearts. Robert Raines writes, "Living the questions of life may be a more realistic and faithful style of Christian living than seeking answers to those questions. . . . Questions are more specific and vital connections with reality than answers could possibly be" (Raines, 1975, p. 11).

Teaching and learning in hospitable environments mean living our questions in community and seeking to discover ways in which the scripture speaks to help us. Creating this kind of environment entails caring without making decisions for another; it means loving enough to nudge and confront as well as to support and comfort. It involves affirming learning accomplished in other times and places, as well as holding out the exciting possibility of future learning. Hospitable space offers tolerance, forgiveness, and affirmation. It requires honesty, accountability, and mutual trust.

Whatever the physical environment, it is the task of those who engage in teaching and learning to be purposeful about building this free and fearless space. We must offer options. We need to discover avenues to think, feel, see, analyze, explore, experiment, hear, express, and create. We do not all have to approach a task in the same way; we do not all have to come to the same conclusions. Agreeing to disagree and being open to learning from those who see the world differently and have beliefs that vary from ours are a mark of a truly hospitable space.

Hospitable environments are not always comfortable ones. They seek to open us up, to encourage us to risk. They foster growth. Growth may be painful, but hospitable environments urge us on.

Name the demons—those stereotypes and realities in our

lives that make us less than God intends we should be. Take them out and examine them. Choose to cast them out in God's name. Being in community means there are those who care for each of us and will pray with and for us. Together all can journey toward wholeness.

Hospitable environments do not hold human beings hostage. Rather, they nurture and support each person. Because people are nurtured, they grow and change. Change sometimes means that it is necessary for the hospitable learning and worshiping community to bless persons and send them out because it is time for them to be in another place. Saying goodbye is as much an act of hospitality as saying, "Welcome to this place, in God's name!"

Adults who dare to live in the world, to be open to the power of God's Spirit, and to share their journey in community with others may discover "the rhythm that makes life human" (Guzie, 1981, p. 18) as they confront life's questions in fellowship around the table that God prepares.

Guides for Those Who Teach

We have begun looking at the story of Jesus feeding the multitude as a way of understanding what it means to serve as a guide for persons on journeys of faith. As a Christian religious educator, I would like to offer some reflections that I believe may guide those who teach and learn in communities of faith. This guidance grows out of my own understandings as a Christian but is offered to all persons of faith. It is my hope that these suggestions can be a beginning point, as you consider and revise them to make them faithfully reflect your own faith and life.

To be a person of faith, as we have seen, we must be *in touch with the world.*

1. *We must be informed and involved in our local, national, and global communities.* Political and economic issues cannot be left to politicians and economists. Decisions to spend more on armaments directly affect benefits available to children, the elderly, and the poor. The quality and availability of education and health care are matters of faith as well as citizenship. Being a faithful

disciple has as much to do with what we do in our work, our families, our leisure, and our communities when we are apart from our faith community as it does with what we do when we are there.

2. *We must draw on the expertise and wisdom of all in the community of faith in order to better understand the complexity of issues facing the world.* The day when teachers may be expected to know all the answers is past. Those who teach must be open and must invite everyone to share their knowledge and expertise. When members of our community do not have the necessary knowledge or experience, we must bring in from the outside those who do.

3. *We must create liaisons with people who are committed to the same issues and work toward peace and justice in the world with them in cooperative ways.* Being in touch with the world means that we will build networks and that we do not need to accomplish everything alone or receive all the credit. Cooperation must extend to other faith communities and beyond.

To be a person of faith one must be *in touch with God.*

1. *Faith is a gift from God; it establishes a relationship and manifests itself in believing, trusting, and acting.* God's gift (grace) comes to us as we worship and serve. For Christians it comes with power through the eucharist. Persons who teach need to be integrally involved in the worship life of the community of faith.

2. *Scripture is a primary means we have for knowing and responding to God's covenant love.* As teachers we have a responsibility to study the scriptures, to know our faith story, and to be able to share the story in appropriate ways.

3. *Recognizing God at work in the world and in our own lives is necessary to remain in touch with God.* It is important for teachers to be able to share their own story. This requires knowing the language to speak behind the wall as well as being able to communicate at the wall with those who do not yet know the community's language.

4. *Being open to the power of God's Spirit at work in us and in the world in ways beyond what we can imagine guards us against trivializing (our understanding of) God.* Being in touch with God prepares us for wonderful surprises. God works in marvelous and mysterious ways, and those who teach need to be open to this reality.

5. *Being touched by God who is love and compassion and mystery endows us with freedom to become all God would have us be.* Fear is no longer in control of those who would teach and learn with pilgrims who share their journeys of faith. Risk and imagination become vehicles for those who would grow in faith. The need to conform or to expect others to conform is replaced with the assurance that God's call comes in many forms and invites us to respond in many different ways. Diversity becomes something to be celebrated rather than despised. Mystery becomes something to be embraced even when it cannot be understood.

Creating a hospitable space for people of faith who choose to learn is an important task for those who accept the call to teach.

1. *The physical environment is important and must be as suitable and as inviting as is possible.* Giving attention to the physical setting where people gather to study and learn does matter. Within the limitations of what is available, the space should be clean, comfortable, and conducive to encouraging all persons to both speak and listen. Whatever we can do to foster dialogue is desirable.

2. *The social and emotional environment is vitally important and should be welcoming, affirming, and safe.* People need a place where they can be honest about who they are and pose their most troubling questions. They need to know that there are no stupid questions and that any question, seriously asked, deserves a serious response (even if there does not seem to be an answer).

3. *The social and emotional atmosphere should be one that enables people to confront and move beyond their assumptions and beliefs.* It is possible for environments to be too comfortable so that people are not challenged to grow and change. A sense of security is actually a prerequisite for human beings to risk considering thinking and acting in different ways. Reframing questions and creating alternative responses are possible in an environment that holds confirmation, contradiction, and continuity in creative tension.

4. *The teaching and learning environment that is appropriate for some persons and groups may not be suitable for all.* It is necessary to involve the group in setting boundaries and expanding horizons so that where you teach and learn together is safe and

hospitable. When some need to move to a different environment, their going needs to be respected.

5. *Environments are not static and fixed; rather, they evolve and change.* Those who assume the role of teacher need to be active about taking responsibility (and encouraging the group to take responsibility) to achieve an appropriate environment and then to maintain and change it as the situation requires. The atmosphere (physical, emotional, social) where people teach and learn requires constant monitoring.

Returning to our opening story, we are reminded that Jesus recognized the necessity of being in touch with the world. The actions of rulers and religious leaders and unnamed pilgrims on a journey were of concern to him and affected his life and ministry. But Jesus recognized that he (and all of us) will be overwhelmed if we do not take time to reflect and to nourish our relationship with our Creator God. Christians are called to accept the nourishment that is available through scripture, prayer, worship, and the eucharist. Being in touch with God (and being touched by God) changes our perspective on the world and gives us strength to address its needs. Finally, we must prepare a place before we can feed the multitude. A safe, hospitable, open space where we are able to be vulnerable and share is required if there is to be food for all.

One way of connecting nine dots with four straight lines:

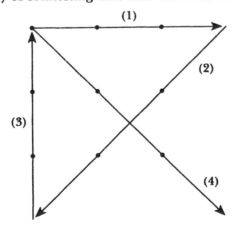

SIX

The Teacher
as Guide
and Companion

Once, in a dry time, Howard Thurman asked me: "What do
you want, Sam? What are your dreams?" He had previously
warned me about the proper order of . . . priorities. "The
first question an individual must ask is 'What is my journey?' Only then is it safe to ask the second question: 'Who
will go with me?' If you get the questions out of order, you
will get in trouble."

—Keen, 1983, p. 172

Those who teach need to ask themselves these questions prior to
undertaking religious education. Are we on the road we want to be
on, headed in the direction we want to go? Do we expect to find
truth in this faith community that we believe can help us make
sense of what is and move toward our vision of what can be? Are
we ready to engage truth as we discover it and as it is revealed to
us? Do we want to commit our being and doing to the truth as we
come to know it? Affirmative responses to questions like these mean
that we are ready to join others in journeying in faith and that we
can assume the role of guide and companion on the way.

We have seen in the story of Jesus feeding the multitude that

People of faith are called to be
in touch with the world
as well as
in touch with God.
By
creating a hospitable space

we are now ready to discover how this story affirms that God's Word touches the world.

God's Word Touches the World

For Christians God's Word is known most fully in the incarnation. Jesus Christ embodies God's self-giving love and shows us the way to wholeness. God's Word comes to us in many other ways, as well—in creation, through the faithfulness of God to the covenant even when we are unfaithful; in the Law, through the words and acts of the prophets; in the power of the Spirit, working in and through persons and nations; and in church, when they are faithful to God's call.

In the accounts of Jesus feeding the multitude, we discover that, even though he was tired and grief stricken, Jesus welcomed the people, healed those who needed healing, and talked with them about the Kingdom of God (Luke 9:11). Jesus demonstrates that God's Word comes to those who seek it in many ways and at their points of need.

God's Word touches the world in ways unknown to us, as well. When we acknowledge the mystery and awesomeness of God, we are ready to be surprised by God's presence and power in places and people that we might never imagine. Knowing God through Jesus Christ calls us to a new humility and frees us to be open to God's Spirit wherever and whenever we are blessed to encounter it.

God's Word comes to us through story and festivity; it appears in our life together as communities of faith seeking to embody faithful living in the world. That story and festivity affirm us, raise questions with which we must struggle, and invite us to see and hear with new eyes and ears so that we are able to incorporate the faith story into our own stories in deeper and more inclusive ways. Our life stories are affirmed and seen in new ways, and pushed beyond our understanding so that we (and our stories) are transformed. Scripture and tradition are primary expressions of the Christian community's Story. The ritual acts of Passover and eucharist are primary examples of festivity for Jews and Christians.

Transformation is a gift from the creating God. Remembering is crucial, as our stories and our faith story intersect and we celebrate. Remembering may be the first step toward claiming the community's faith story as our own and joining in the festivity with our faith family (Grierson, 1984, p. 55). Making the story our own leads us to committed living, as we seek to respond in faith to the graciousness of God's love. When we respond, we are blessed and "upheld by a power we do not control, promising a fulfillment not of what we have crafted, but of what the giver of grace continually crafts through us, with us, and despite us" (Brown, 1980, p. 80). That is what seems to have happened to many who followed Jesus to a lonely place.

Of course, the process does not always occur in the same way. Remembering, claiming the Story, and committed living are all given birth and nurtured by God's gracious love, even as they draw us ever more toward God's reign and realm of inclusive love. Sometimes we claim the Story as a result of committed living. Sometimes remembering the story leads us into faithful living.

We should also recognize the danger that people may convince themselves that they can claim the faith, even though it is neither based in their memory, nor celebrated, nor lived. The church contributes to this deception whenever it baptizes children of parents who no longer remember, participate in worship, or seek to live in faith.

Glimpses of God's Perspective

Have you ever seen a map that places North America at the center of the world? "The effect—besides moving the center of the world from Greenwich to the longitude of Peoria, Illinois—is to leave Japan and a chunk of eastern Asia visible on the west with the

remainder of a truncated Asia reappearing far, again, in the east. . . .
The literal-minded school[child], shown this map and asked to
define the 'Far East' would look carefully and reply: 'Iran, Pakistan,
and Afghanistan'. . . . If Iran and Pakistan become the 'Far East',
then surely this . . . places the 'Near East' smack down on the Place
de la Concorde and Piccadilly Circus" (Isaacs, 1958, pp. 42–43).

How often we assume that we have "God's map" in our
possession and that the way we view the world is the correct way.
We can smile at the ethnocentrism that this North American–centered map illustrates. But it inspires us to look at the deep truth that
God's perspective is not the same as our own. We see the world in
ways that reflect our own origins, ethnicity, race and class, nationality, and the faiths of our birth and our communities. That is inevitable. The problem comes when we assume that God is on our side
and sees the world as we see it. And that cannot be, for God is the
creator of the universe who is not bound by time or space or
finiteness.

In the accounts of the feeding of the multitude, we discover
that the disciples' perspective was very different from that of their
rabbi. "Sending the people away," which seemed the only option
to the disciples, is transformed into "giving them something to eat,"
because Jesus' perspective reflects the graciousness of God.

What we are given is glimpses into God's perspective that
expand our horizons and open us up to truths that we are only now
capable of grasping. Those who are open to seeing with new eyes
and who accept the responsibility on behalf of the faith community
to be a guide and companion for others should heed Harris's advice
to learners to " 'Accept no dogma without investigation, it might
be wrong,' as well as to 'Reject no dogma without investigation, it
might be right' " (Harris, 1989b, p. 116).

Because both Jewish and Christian religious education are by
definition communal activities, those who teach have the responsibility of helping those on the journey "explore the often contradictory and ambiguous nexus where private troubles and public issues
meet" (Brookfield, 1987, p. 62). God's perspective is too broad for
us to separate personal concerns from national and global problems. God's perspective encompasses all of life: need, creed, and

deed. Our faith response requires "(1) a belief conviction, (2) a trusting relationship, and (3) a lived life of agape" (Groome, 1980, p. 57).

God's perspective is conveyed in many ways. A primary way for Christians is through scripture. When we open ourselves to scripture we often find in God's Word "unexpected news" (see Brown, 1984). Those who hear and receive the gospel of Jesus are often accused of being the "people who have been turning the world upside down" and who "are acting contrary to the decrees of the emperor" (Acts 17:6b–7). But turning the world upside down or attacking institutions does not automatically assure that we are seeing the world as God sees it. Whether or not we are acting in harmony with God's perspective (for that is the most we can hope to do) is to be measured by the "fruits of the Spirit—love, joy, peace, patience, kindness, generosity, faithfulness, gentleness, and self-control" (Gal. 6:22–23a). Faithfulness calls Christians to be disciples (learners) of Jesus Christ who rejoice in and work toward the all-inclusive and just reign and realm of God. Fruits of the Spirit are seen as necessary in all world religions.

Breaking Bread

How often in the gospels (Matthew, Mark, Luke, and John) we read of powerful and life-transforming experiences occurring as people participated in the breaking of bread. Certainly, breaking bread transformed the multitude and the two disciples who had traveled from Jerusalem to Emmaus. We also see its power as Jesus' feet were washed with tears as he prepared to share a meal with the Pharisees, as he celebrated the Passover meal with his disciples in the upper room, and when he shared breakfast on the shore with his disciples after the resurrection.

The Hebrew scriptures also emphasize the sacramental nature of shared meals. We find Abraham and Sarah offering hospitality to the messengers from God who announced (at table) that Sarah would have a child. God provided manna in the wilderness to sustain weary travelers, and the focus of the Passover celebration is a feast. For Asian Christians today, sharing rice is a powerful way of speaking about being "at table" (Takenaka, 1986).

Jim Wallis understands the centrality of breaking bread for

Christian communities when he says, "Around the Eucharist table we come again and again to be healed, reconciled, and sent forth whole" (1983, p. 101). Breaking bread is at the very heart of Christian community. It is an everyday, ordinary experience that is transformed and made sacred; through it we are endowed with grace as we share at table with our brothers and sisters in Christ. We are blessed, and our hunger is satisfied—but not because we are better than others; we are called into a serving ministry so that the whole world might also come to accept the invitation to receive God's gracious love and be made whole.

Christian teaching and learning that are cut off from this sacramental act cannot be all that they are meant to be. The eucharist offers to all who will come "a foretaste of that just Kingdom where all will be accorded their due" (White, 1983, p. 110). As Reinhold Niebuhr said, it is "the mystery which makes sense out of life always threatened by meaninglessness" (Niebuhr, 1984, p. 1197).

"Sacrament is 'God's self giving' (White), 'doors to the sacred' (Martos), 'visible words' (Jenson), 'presence of God calling us to presence' (Duffy), 'life in all its totality—returned to [us], given again as sacrament' (Schmemann), 'the celebration of our new enlightenment and interpretation . . . translated into gestures and signs that signify our discovery' (Segundo), 'Spirit-filled signs that actually effect here and now for us the very thing we are celebrating' (Bausch)" (Browning and Reed, 1985, p. 120). Christians understand sacrament to be the gift God offers to all who believe and choose to become members of the body of Christ. It is the gift the church has to offer to a chaotic and hungry world as we invite others to come to the banquet (see Nouwen, 1986, pp. 88–89).

Festivity grows out of living the Christian life and sharing its story. Guzie claims that "story *names* our lived experience" while "festivity *frames* it" (1981, p. 20). The frame without the picture is useless. So it is that any of our festive celebrations that do not grow out of the Christian life are meaningless and sometimes destructive. Some New Year's Eve celebrations are one illustration of empty, lifeless festivity. Participating in Passover or eucharist without remembering and claiming the story as one's own also lacks significance.

Sacraments can be understood as festive actions that Christians perform as they acknowledge "their lived experience" and "*call to heart* their common story" (Guzie, 1981, p. 130—emphasis mine). The sacraments are alive. Sharing in the celebration of the sacraments (especially eucharist and baptism) "creates community and, at the same time, community that already exists is made stronger by becoming concrete and visible" (White, 1983, pp. 30–31).

Brown reminds us that sacraments show us "for a single moment the way [life] is supposed to be in all moments" (1980, p. 18). Sacrament can be a taste of what we are called to make of all life's experiences. Christians are called to sacramental living that reflects God's gracious love in everything that is said and done (Brown, 1980).

In the accounts of the feeding of the multitude, the gospel writers remind us that it is in the blessing, breaking, and sharing of bread that God's grace is mediated to those who accept the invitation to eat and be filled. "Understood as communion, the sacrament is given to make real the fellowship and family of God to which all men and women are called to belong and so be at home and be sustained in their journeying through the process of life to the realized fellowship of love which is the kingdom of God" (Jenkins, 1990, p. 174).

Sharing with Disciples Who Share

It is important to remember that Jesus did not feed the multitude. Rather, he asked his disciples to give the food that he had blessed to those who were hungry. The community of faith needs disciples who will enable the whole community to share what they have with one another and with the hungry.

Teachers are called to be such disciples. Teachers have the responsibility of providing access to the faith community's story and traditions. Boys suggests that this means "to erect bridges, to make metaphors, to build highways, to provide introductions and commentaries, to translate foreign terms, to remove barriers, to make maps, to demolish blockages, to demonstrate effects, to energize and sustain participation, and to be hospitable" (1989a, p. 209).

In a book on mentoring, Daloz reminds us that it is necessary for us and for those we guide to journey into our "dark side" in order to become whole, for "wholeness is a far more precious gift than perfection" (1986, p. 153). I believe that knowing who and whose we are requires recognizing that we are both sinful and redeemed children of God. We Christians are free precisely because we are not bound by the need to be perfect; we have been set free by God's gracious gift of salvation and can journey toward that just reign and realm of God as our grateful response to the gift we have been given. The journey is one that invites (even requires) that we share this good news of God's gift.

We have already said that teaching is in large part the asking of probing questions. Sharing does not mean giving others our answers. Answers that satisfy need to be born out of the living and struggling of those who seek them. The final product is not so valuable as the process that leads us through the desert and to the oasis. Those who are not thirsty are less receptive to what the oasis has to offer.

Answering someone else's questions on the basis of our own experience or another external source is "a bit like flying a group of hikers to the top of the mountain when one person's reason for the trip is to learn to climb, another's to collect wild flowers, and another's simply to enjoy the day." Instead, we may be called upon to share "a good story [which] is a kind of hologram of the life of an individual, a culture, or a whole species. Each of us hears in it, with ears conditioned by our own history, what we most need at the time to understand" (Daloz, 1986, p. 24).

Those who teach are blessed as they share. There really is truth in the often-quoted claim, "Those who teach learn the most of all!" Cox asserts that his faith "grows and deepens" most "when [he acts] on it and when [he tries] to give it to someone else" (1983, p. 158).

It is necessary to remember that those with whom we share must be given freedom to receive, explore, question, challenge, accept, hold in abeyance, or reject all that we suggest. Being a companion and guide on the journey must not involve coercion or manipulation. Gifts that are not freely accepted have little value. Patience is one of the primary attributes required of those who act as guide and companion to others on the journey.

Both the Hebrew scriptures and the New Testament affirm

over and over again that the call to commitment always carries with it the right (even the responsibility) for each person in each generation to make a conscious choice—"choose this day whom you will serve" (Josh. 23). Trusting the Holy Spirit to direct and change others as they are ready to receive is one of the hardest things for many teachers to do.

Those of us who accept the privilege and responsibility of guide and companion to others seeking to respond to God's call must reexamine our own understandings and the language we use as we seek to be faithful disciples. Daloz suggests that if we see ourselves as "covering certain topics," "giving certain information," "building skills," and "shaping behavior," we may be viewing our students "as vessels to be filled or inert objects to be molded" rather than seeking to "respect the organic quality of growth in our students" (Daloz, 1986, pp. 240-241).

Those who are providing us with maternal and feminist images to counteract the mechanistic, production-orientated, dominating images that pervade our culture suggest that we think of teaching as a dance—and of "awakening," "discovering," "creating," "dwelling," "nourishing," "traditioning," and "transforming" as steps to the dance (Harris, 1989a). Inviting others to join in the circle acknowledges the need to celebrate and mourn (dances of mourning can be powerfully releasing and freeing) during the journey.

Being a guide and companion is both gift and responsibility. It requires us to listen to God (through the reading of scripture, prayer, worship, and dialogue with others) and to those who travel with us. It requires us to be willing to reframe questions and to be open when our assumptions about the best way of journeying are challenged. Faithful teaching requires a "stance of receptivity, of attunement, of listening" (Daloz, 1986, p. 244). Teaching "sharpens and magnifies our sense of contradiction" as we become more aware of all the ways "the wholeness of the Spirit contrasts dramatically with the brokenness of our persons and our world." Those who teach are called to be an example of "living the contradictions" (Palmer, 1979, p. 8).

The mission of the church—the body of Christ—calls all Christians to engage in sacramental living so that the faith community becomes "a sacrament to the Kingdom" (Groome, 1980, p. 50). The church is called to witness to the gift of abundant life that God offers to us all.

More Than Enough for All

Many in developed nations are used to thinking in terms of a market economy, where demand and supply are interrelated and shortages (both real and created) lead persons to hoard what they fear may not be available in the future. It is precisely this kind of thinking that God rejects. In the account of the feeding of the multitude, Jesus creates an environment where people are able to put aside their selfishness; and to the astonishment of everyone—including the disciples—there is more than enough to go around.

One of the major blocks to accepting what Jesus teaches us here and what the Hebrew prophets proclaim is the feverish consumerism that is destroying people who have access to resources and power and threatens the rest of the world, which has seen enough to want its fair share of "goods and services." Advertising bombards us every day with the message that enough is *not* enough, and good is *never* good enough. Unless we, as people of faith, can break the bonds of consumerism, we will never be able to claim the promise that there really *is* more than enough for all.

We can never forget what happened to Jesus (and what often happens to those who truly follow in his way). When all are invited to the table to share the eucharistic feast, there is present a source of power that can change the world; also present is "a condemnation of false confidence in any existing society as it falls short of that Kingdom God wills to bring about" (White, 1983, p. 110). There is more than enough for all if and when we, as members of the body of Christ, use the power that comes with *giving* rather than taking, with *serving* rather than controlling, with *becoming instruments* of God through the power of the Spirit rather than relying on "principalities and powers."

Gathering the Leftovers

After all those pilgrims were fed, and when they were satisfied, "what was left over was gathered up, twelve baskets of broken pieces" (Luke 9:17). Commentaries suggest that collecting the left-overs was a normal practice at the conclusion of a meal. Yet readers are struck by the realization that there was more food after everyone had eaten their fill than when Jesus blessed the loaves and fishes that were distributed to the multitude.

For those who find in this event an example for being a guide and companion, the message seems clear. It is not enough to create and organize the environment in order to provide hospitable space where teaching and learning can occur; it is not enough to have a plan to address the issues at hand. We also need a way of drawing to a close and assessing what has happened and what remains to be done. Resources for future learning and teaching must not be wasted.

It is interesting to note that none of the gospel accounts report on the crowds' reaction to what was experienced that day. It was enough to say that the people were fed. But Jesus did explain to the disciples why he chose to act as he did. We find this explanation in two parallel accounts of the "feeding of the four thousand" (Matt. 15:32; Mark 8:2-3), where Jesus both acts as an example and seeks to help his disciples understand what the good news is and how and why we are to share it.

Tools for Adult Religious Educators

What tools do we need if we accept the responsibility of being guide and companion? Which ones will serve us and all who journey with us faithfully and well?

First, it seems clear that the Bible must be a basic tool; scripture is the substance of the stories and the teachings that we must hear and try to understand and make our own. It *invites* all to meet and to enter into a covenant relationship with God; it *sends us out* to be the "salt of the earth" and "lights to the nations," as we share the good news that God is love and desires to redeem all human beings.

But those who accept the privileges and responsibilities of being guide and companion should not attempt to interpret the scriptures for those on the journey. Rather, teachers must offer other tools so that others can understand the biblical message for themselves. There are many ways of teaching and learning the Bible. A wide range of resources and approaches to scripture study are helpful (see Chapter Eight for specific resources).

No one resource or approach is right for everyone or for any one person all of the time. We need to find ways to help persons overcome their fixed ideas about what the Bible says and to experience it in new ways. There is not time to read a passage, verse by verse, and then have someone announce what it means. Bible study requires us to encounter the Word, to be open to understanding its context, to struggle with its message in light of the present situation, and to test our understandings against the thrust of the whole biblical message, tradition, our own and our faith community's religious experiences, and reason. Those who teach need to be ready

1. To tell the stories of the faith community that relate to the journey struggles of persons who are seeking to learn;
2. To assist all who are sharing in the journey in learning to use tools for Bible study;
3. To create thought-provoking questions that help the group move beyond the status quo in order to think in more inclusive ways; and
4. To remain open and eager to learn everything possible from those who have joined us on the journey.

Second, those who truly share their faith journeys and seek to grow and learn together become a *caring community* of pilgrims. Teaching and learning opportunities need to develop and incorporate ritual acts that strengthen a feeling of oneness. Ritual acts reflect and reinforce the care we offer to one another. A learning community's sense of identity and continuity grows out of its ritual life and can sustain both individuals and groups during times of crisis and loss.

As we have seen, a primary ritual act in the church is the celebration of eucharist. Learning communities must have opportunities to share this feast together. Eucharist can be celebrated as groups begin or complete a particular study, at a New Year's Eve watch-night party, or at the beginning or conclusion of each study session. Finding appropriate times to break bread together—both in the celebration of the eucharist and in the sharing of meals—unites people and builds trust that enables them to speak and listen in a way that can transform the group and individual lives.

There are many other events and experiences that we should acknowledge, celebrate, or even mourn. Foster maintains that rituals can be created for all of life's milestones. Rituals are created when (1) the group names and focuses on a particular experience or person, (2) there is a group response, (3) a blessing is given, and (4) there is a response from the person who has been named or who can respond to the situation.

Christmas, Good Friday, Easter, Pentecost, Passover, bar and bat mitzvahs, Rosh Hashanah, birthdays, promotions, the loss of jobs, moves, important moments or crises in the lives of our children and parents, marriages, divorces, illnesses, and deaths are examples of the times when we need to share in ritual acts. These ritual acts are not "extras" that make a group feel good; they should be an integral part of the life of the group and as much a part of what it means to study and learn together as Bible and topical studies (see Foster, 1986, pp. 47–49).

Third, teachers who become guides and companions must develop both skills and insights that can only come through *prayerful, thoughtful teaching.* We must always recognize that God's Spirit is at work in persons (including *us*) and ways beyond our imagination and that time spent in prayer is as crucial as time spent in teaching preparation.

Because we *know* and at the same time *know that we do not know all,* there is a freedom to be vulnerable, to trust that God is at work in the process as well as in the faith story, and to claim the promise that God's grace is sufficient. We are freed from the burden that we are somehow responsible for the decisions of those we teach. We can admit that we do not have all the answers. We can offer a hospitable, challenging environment and process, listen to those with whom we journey, seek faithfully to share the Story, and enter into the life of the learning community with authenticity. This sense that truth is what we all seek together gives those who journey with us the real freedom to discern for themselves what God is calling them to do and be.

To attempt to be open to the myriad ways that adults teach

and learn must also be part of our praying and reflecting. For example, it took me a long time to recognize that some teachers have a clear sense of what they are hoping to have happen in a class only when they have finished their teaching-learning plan. Not everyone is helped by having a clearly stated objective before they begin their planning.

How we think and organize will be very varied. The ways we create the environment and orchestrate the process of teaching and learning need to make both those who learn as we do and those whose learning styles are very different feel comfortable. To accomplish the goal requires prayer and reflection that is in tune with God through the Spirit and with the needs and desires of those with whom we journey. Unless we *know* ourselves, God, and our companions, we will not be faithful guides.

We need to ask ourselves what we would expect from a guide if we were climbing a dangerous mountain peak. I would want someone who knew the territory—who would not be misled when we came to forks in the path. I would want someone who understood the seasons, weather conditions, and human nature and someone who could make reasoned decisions about when to begin and when to take refuge in a sheltered area. The guide should be able to make wise decisions about what we need to carry with us and what we should leave behind. My guide would need to be wise: to know when to take risks and when prudence was the better course.

I would not want my guide to hurry me unduly or to pamper me unnecessarily. I would expect that person to challenge me to develop greater skills in and understanding of climbing; I would be expected to carry my weight and to be responsible to the total group of climbers. The guide I would choose would hold me and my companions accountable so that we might all reach our destination safely.

All these things being equal, I would also hope my guide would have a love of nature and the gift to see beauty along the way, a sense of humor that would lighten an otherwise serious and dangerous climb, and an awareness that the quality of the journey is at least as important as reaching our destination.

Much is required of those who agree to guide others: knowledge and wisdom, skills and understanding of how to engage others in the processes of learning, and the ability to trust and be trusted. The teacher must also be able to discern when to push and when to comfort, when to chastise and when to praise, when to challenge and when to hold back, when to encourage risk and when to protect.

Being a gifted asker of questions, having the patience to wait while others discover answers for themselves, and sharing leadership without abdicating responsibility foster growth of both individuals and groups. Knowing that our call is to be faithful, and that we do not need to know and cannot measure the fruits of our teaching frees us from the bondage of "popularity and success." There is a sense of deep peace in claiming the promise that wholeness is a gift and that the appropriate response is faithfulness and not perfection.

Summarizing a Model for Teaching and Learning
Based on the Gospel Accounts of the Feeding of the Multitude

We have seen in the story of Jesus feeding the multitude that

People of faith are called to be
in touch with the world
as well as
in touch with God.
By
creating a hospitable space,
people discover that
God's Word touches the world.
By being open to
glimpses of God's perspective
that are celebrated in the
breaking of bread,
people begin
sharing with disciples who, in turn, share
in ways that offer
more than enough for all.
People of faith are asked to
gather the leftovers
as they participate in God's all-inclusive, justice-seeking
reign and realm that both is and is coming to be.

PART THREE

Strengthening Religious Education Experiences

This section considers tools that adult religious education can offer to communities of faith. Chapter Seven offers a foundation for creating models for faith communities that want people to know and claim their faith story and grow toward more faithful living. It is a foundation that holds possibilities for Christian religious education and is offered to religious educators of other faith communities who are committed to an openness to truth and who seek a more just and humane world. Chapter Eight examines ways of developing programs for adult religious education in communities of faith attempting to embody their own models. Chapter Nine assesses approaches to teaching and learning and suggests methods that may be useful for those who teach adults in faith communities. Chapter Ten shows ways of making connections, sharing power, and reaching out to those outside our own faith communities so that we can begin talking and working with those with whom we share a vision for justice and peace. It outlines strategies for those who seek to journey through adulthood in faith.

SEVEN

Developing
a New Vision
for Adult
Religious Education

The vast majority of people make choices more out of the myths they live than out of the abstract principles they have learned. That is why it is so essential to become aware of the *stories* we live, the *larger stories* which we daily tap into and which give us the real backdrop for our most personal choices, good or bad.

—Guzie, 1981, p. 15—emphasis mine

Knowing the Story: Experiencing the Past

Both Jews and Christians are a part of a "story-formed community" (Westerhoff, 1984, p. 1). It is through the stories of our faith, our nation, our ancestors, and our families and through our own stories (which evolve from our experiences) that we know who we are and why we act as we do. There is immense power in those stories we choose to remember, for they serve as "lenses through which we understand life" and guide our decision making. It is out of stories that our values are formed; stories "re-energize our commitment" to both do and be (Morgan, 1986, p. 7).

Stories "are always more important than facts" because they have power to involve us, to move us into a world beyond our own knowledge, to censure our attitudes and beliefs, and to transform us. Stories always exist first and are the basis for traditions and the forming of communities. Stories "precede and produce" communities of faith; theologies are "rooted in and flow from [their] story" (Bausch, 1984, pp. 195–199).

It is crucial to understand that there is not *one* story for any faith community. The Hebrew Bible offers the perspectives of those who wanted a king and those who were opposed. It provides varying judgments about leaders, events, and practices from the points of view of priests and prophets; the opinions of those from the northern kingdom differ from those from the southern kingdom. For Christians there are four gospels, not one. It seems clear that even core, community-forming stories are "open-ended" and "conditioned by the assumptions and frame of references of their times" (Bausch, 1984, p. 199). The perspective of the writer of the gospel of John differs from the author of Mark. People seeking to know the story of Jesus' life and ministry have a fuller understanding because they are able to see through the eyes of both John and Mark.

We do violence to story when we seek to make it literal. "History is the bridge from which we view the story in all its forms and in all its aspects of truth." History can save us from either idolizing story or making it so irrelevant that it is lost (Bausch, 1984, p. 199).

Story that is the foundation of faith communities is "God's recreative story," which both grounds and transforms those who know and experience it (Westerhoff, 1984, p. 2). As "open story" it is never finished and can take those in faith communities "on a journey toward the mysteries of human existence held in common" (Williams, 1979, p. 7).

Stories that challenge our world views, raise questions about our interpretations of life, and emphasize those areas we would rather not explore become parables that challenge us to question and expand our world. Jesus used parables in ways that transformed stories and people. Story is able to offer us paradoxes that succeed in "catching us off guard, sneaking by our defenses, and opening us up to unexpected mystery" (Bausch, 1984, p. 79).

It is precisely those biblical stories that will not allow us to ignore the "pain and promise, . . . the need for repentance, . . . and the possibility of conversion" that persons in Christian faith communities need to hear in new ways—and also to understand from the perspective of the poor and marginalized. The core stories of both Christians and Jews "confront, threaten, or challenge people of power, people for whom God's word is first a word of judgment and perhaps later one of possibility" (Nelson-Pallmeyer, 1989, p. 75).

The first task for those who would create models for engaging adults in teaching and learning is to tell, sing, retell, and ritualize the "old, old stories," so that people are able to see themselves in the stories and make them their own. Christian theologians from oppressed nations and groups and postholocaust Jews demonstrate how our faith stories can shed light on our present situations in powerful ways (see Pobee and von Wartenberg-Potter (1986), Takenaka (1986), Tamez (1982), Herzberger (1983), and von Wartenberg-Potter (1988); see also the writings of Chaim Potok and Elie Wiesel). Telling and retelling in ways that connect to current life experiences and ritualizing our faith stories are what all persons of faith are called to do.

It is out of the stories of faith communities that people receive an "incarnational view of life." As they encounter mystery, story is born. Through story, people of faith create the world in which they live, relate, and make choices. As Moses confronted "I am who I am, I will be who I will be" in the burning bush, the Jewish people were being formed and reformed into a community of faith. As Saul's experience of blindness "opened his eyes," the Christian community was being shaped and reshaped. As Jews and Christians today know and experience their faith stories in their own lives, they, too, can be transformed (Seymour, O'Gorman, and Foster, 1984, pp. 138–139). Without hearing and being able to remember faith stories from the past, human beings cannot make vital connections to faith communities.

Faith stories offer us a context out of which to make sense of all of life; they offer us images and words that help us to interpret, to make decisions, and to try to move forward. For Christians, the faith story is the embodiment in Jesus Christ of God's gracious love for the whole creation.

Understanding the tradition is a process of getting inside the core story so that it becomes our story to be owned, revised, and lived in faithful discipleship. The Christian Tradition has been described by the conference on faith and order of the World Council of Churches as "the gospel itself, transmitted from generation to generation in and by the church, Christ . . . present in the life of the church"; traditions may be understood as the ways different cultures and church communities understand the central Tradition (Merritt, 1990, p. 182).

It is an essential task of those who would journey in faith to know and understand their roots; each person and faith community can then make wise decisions about where they should tap and where they need to prune and graft to provide nourishment for the journey. Traditions can be overpowering and controlling or they can be helpful and liberating. But they are necessary for the survival of communities of faith. We cannot change what we do not identify and claim.

It is the faith community's responsibility to engage the Christian tradition in ways that liberate and to reject using traditions to control and enslave. Moore (1983) describes a "traditioning model of education," which is "a process by which God's gifts are received and passed on, not as a static box of things, but as dynamic life-changing events" (p. 121). It is crucial that we grasp the significance of the reality that God not only acted in the past, but that God acts in the present and will act in the future. Traditioning leads us to see that we are involved in the "stream of history"; the faith community's tradition becomes the expression—through beliefs, actions, rituals, and values—of who the community has been, is, and will become (Moore, 1983, pp. 121–146).

Writing about Jewish religious education, Sherry Blumberg and Eugene Borowitz advocate an open presentation and exploration of ideas about God in the context of reverence toward life and faith. In this way people can be nurtured in ways that hold together past, present, and future in order to "model to the students that religious expression in all of its diversity involves the mind, body, spirit, and feelings of a whole human being" (Blumberg and Borowitz, 1988, p. 219).

Educators who turn their backs on the need for people to know the story and to experience the past run the risk of the rapid demise of their faith community. It has been observed that "a grandparent's animating beliefs to a child's imitation of parental practice to a grandchild's indifference" is a three-generation road toward the loss of the vitality and viability of faith. Each generation must encounter the living God as those in preceding generations have done, on its own terms and in relation to its own life situations (Maitland, 1985, p. 116).

Knowing the story and experiencing the past prepares human beings to encounter the living God by

1. Telling, retelling, singing, ritualizing, and celebrating the stories of faith so that the core story becomes a part of each person's own story;
2. Teaching them the language of faith—that is, the language behind the wall;
3. Offering eyes for seeing and ears for hearing as they have come to know their ancestors in the faith;
4. Protecting them from the blindness and excesses that may be present at the particular time and place where they find themselves;
5. Discovering a sense of the ongoing nature of God's mighty acts in history and the power of God's faithfulness; and
6. Rediscovering for themselves and their contemporary faith community the power and responsibility that come with being connected with their faith, across the generations and around the world.

Claiming the Story: Living into the Present

> We can only retell and live by the stories we have read or heard. We live our lives through texts. They may be read, or chanted, or experienced electronically, or come to us, like the murmurings of our mothers, telling us what conventions demand. Whatever their form or medium, these stories

> have formed us all; they are what we must use to make new
> fictions, new narratives [Heilbrun, 1988, p. 37].

Here we are in the present, called to be participants in the
living faith tradition in which we find ourselves. It becomes the task
of adult religious education to help persons interpret and reinterpret the stories of the faith tradition as they seek to make sense and
to live faithfully. Praxis (that interactive process of reflecting and
acting, of theory and practice) becomes the means by which persons
live.

Questioning becomes a necessary part of living in the present. We are called to share with Janus (an ancient Roman god of
doorways who had two faces and so always faced both backward and
forward) the responsibility of both conserving what is just and true
from the past while moving toward a more just future. To explore,
to understand, to reform, to create, to transform, and to be transformed are necessary for faithful living.

Living in the present has little in common with existing. It
is active rather than passive; it is rooted in the past and works toward
a justice-seeking future; it requires us to assume responsibility for
thinking about and choosing how we will be and act. We continue
to grow and learn as we engage in praxis, praxis that is informed
by knowing and claiming our past and that is drawn toward a vision
for the future that fosters imagination and creativity.

This does not mean that adults must be adrift in an ocean
of uncertainty. We should recognize that as imaginative and critical
thinkers who engage in praxis we can be both passionate and committed persons of faith. Commitment that has "passed through the
fires of this critical analysis" and that remains open to the possibility of new insight and truth becomes commitment worth living
and dying for (see Brookfield, 1987, pp. 21-23).

As adults it becomes possible to "appreciate the relative, pro-
visional, and contextual nature of public and private knowledge"
and to recognize that our beliefs, values, life-styles reflect our socialization and have been culturally constructed (Brookfield, 1986,
pp. 293-294). It is easy for us who teach about faith to forget that
what we have been taught as a "true" Christian belief is always
someone's interpretation. We are at a time now when quite different

views of faith and history are being expressed. Women, blacks, and the poor and marginalized around the world are beginning to present histories of very different persons and events and interpretations from quite different perspectives.

When we believe that God is truth, we need not fear being open to others' views and to exploring our own doubts and questions. Questioning is what the Hebrews were called to do when they struggled with whether or not they ought to have a king. That is what the early church did when it grappled with what it meant to include Gentiles in its faith community. That is what the church in the United States did when it struggled with the issue of slavery. And that is what faith communities are asked to do today, for example, as they try to understand sexuality and what it means to be a family in a new way.

Living in the present as persons of faith requires us to "make creative contributions to the ongoing unfolding of the drama," as we seek to be faithful to the playwright-director's story line, to acknowledge those actors and dancers who have preceded us, and to "come onto the stage to learn our moves and to awaken to the dance or drama in process" as we "grow in a 'grace-full' fitting of our dance to the larger movement of the core plot." People of faith claim the promise that the author-director is always present and that, no matter what lines are forgotten or what steps are missed, "the whole drama-dance [will continue] toward the climactic fulfillment envisioned by the script" (Fowler, 1984, pp. 137–138).

The present becomes the link in the dynamic connection between the story as it has been embodied in past tradition and the story as it is now and will be transformed in the future (Harris, 1979, pp. 35–57). Taking the present seriously means that it becomes necessary to live toward a realized eschatology rather than clinging to a future (only) eschatology. It grounds us not only in the past but "deeply in the depths of the present. . . . Now is the bringing together of the best of the past and of the future" (Fox, 1983, p. 105). This present can never be understood in only individualistic ways; it is communal. As people who are part of a "story-formed community," we become members of a drama-dance company and are called to work in harmony with all who share in this community and who give allegiance to the playwright-director.

By claiming the Story and accepting the responsibility to live into the present, people of faith are called to

1. Both know the story and be willing to reinterpret and reform it as they seek to be open to understanding and acting in harmony with God's directing and creating power.
2. Question and reflect as active participants in the drama-dance of life.
3. Acknowledge that their understandings of both story and tradition are contextually formed and must always be open to revision in light of the perspectives and experiences of others.
4. Accept that committed faith must be open to new truth whenever and wherever it is revealed so that beliefs, values, and lifestyles can always be altered according to the will of the playwright-director.
5. Participate in their communities of faith so that their understandings and actions are always open to assessment by those who journey with us.

Transforming the Story: Moving into the Future

> This is the mission entrusted to the church, a hard mission: to uproot sins from history, to uproot sins from the political order, to uproot sins from the economy, to uproot sins wherever they are. What a hard task! It has to meet conflicts and so much selfishness, so much pride, so much vanity, so many who have enthroned the reign of sin among us [Archbishop Oscar Romero, quoted in Nelson-Pallmeyer, 1989, p. 73].

When people are content with the way things are and are not experiencing cognitive dissonance, there is not likely to be much desire to change. It is when one's way of knowing or acting is challenged that there is energy to invest in new understandings and ways of acting. There is pain as well as power involved in "perspective transformation" and "paradigm shifting," and these are almost always called forth by some event or experience that challenges our personal and social worlds (Brookfield, 1986, pp. 49–50).

As we have seen, human beings react to stress and cognitive

dissonance in a variety of ways. Some seek to hang on to old ways of knowing and doing. When that is not an option, people may turn to imagination as a way of envisioning alternative futures or to critical reflection, which involves them in evaluating the present and remembering and reexamining the past; they can then explore other visions for the future and ways of moving into that future (Groome, 1980, pp. 185–187).

Transformative education must be both societal and personal and must affect the total self as well as one's environment. It asks us to find ways of infusing Kegan's understanding of confirmation (holding on), contradiction (letting go), and continuity (staying put for reintegration) (1982, pp. 118–120), with Martin's call for gender-sensitive education that focuses on nurturing, caring, concern, and connection for all learners (1985, pp. 193–199). These ideas may help us to face contradiction and confrontation.

For Christians transformation grows out of encounter with Jesus Christ and is an ongoing process. As people receive the gift of God's self-giving love, they are called to live out of love rather than fear, to give rather than to control, to serve rather than to accumulate power or money or possessions, to be open to alternative ways of experiencing and understanding what God calls us to be and do.

Loder suggests that there are two fundamental blocks to that transformative living manifested in self-giving love—the fear that acceptance means losing one's own sense of self and one's beliefs and values and the fear that death will result from being rejected and abandoned (1989, p. 174). When human beings allow themselves to succumb to these fears, transformation is impossible, and they may seek to live in the past or find themselves stuck in a not-very-satisfactory present.

People committed to transforming the story and living into the future must first name the demons that control and block them and institutions from the truth. In this age of misleading euphemisms, we have been reluctant to name reality in direct and straightforward ways. For example, we baptize false gods by calling missiles that have the power to destroy human life and the planet "peacekeepers."

Hosea, Jeremiah, and Jesus called persons to recognize and

name their life-controlling demons and to cast them out. "No faithfulness or loyalty, . . . no knowledge of God, . . . swearing, lying, and murder, and stealing and adultery and . . . bloodshed" (Hos. 4:1–3) are among the demons Hosea names on behalf of God—demons for which prophet, priest, and the whole people are responsible. Experiencing a transformed and transforming story may mean reading the scriptures with new eyes and hearing with new ears; it means accepting the story that judges and challenges as well as claiming the promises that the story brings.

Confronting the idols is the second step. Idolatry and blasphemy are prevalent in affluent cultures, where the shopping mall has become the cathedral and consumerism has become the way to salvation. It is idolatrous when societies that are being buried by their own garbage, strangled by breathing the air that surrounds them, and poisoned by eating the food they have produced and drinking the water they have polluted assume that technology can solve all of their problems. Idols can be found in communities of faith as well as in secular cultures. Whenever human beings are guilty of dehumanizing behavior—racist, sexist, classist, or ageist—in the name of religion, there are false gods to be confronted. Whenever people demean and abuse persons or any form of creation, idols are apt to be present and need to be challenged.

The golden calf that Moses discovered when he came down from the mountain (Exod. 32) becomes a symbol for all the things in which we put our trust and for all the times we fail to rely on the Sovereign One and turn aside to worship and live according to our own needs and understandings. Confronting idols needs to begin in our own lives and faith communities rather than with judging others. It requires self and communal examination and always leads to confession and renewal.

The third step involved in transformation challenges our human tendency to compartmentalize and requires us to make visible connections in every sphere of life. Increasing social services for children, the poor, and the aged entails cutting the military budget. Requiring strict environmental regulations means that life-styles will have to be changed. Faith communities that accept the need to make visible connections will not be able to oversimplify any one issue and deal with it in isolation. Family planning, birth control, abortion, sex education in the schools, AIDS, rape, the criminal justice system, poverty, racism, and capital punishment will have to be studied and responded to in light of larger societal and global contexts.

Amos made connections that the people of Israel did not want to hear. Jesus made connections that linked Samaritans, tax collectors, women, and lepers to God's gracious love in ways that threatened the religious people of his day. People who want to claim that faith is personal and individualistic refuse to see the ties that bind all humankind and all creation. Persons of faith are called to live toward a justice-seeking, all-inclusive family of God where peace with justice becomes real.

Transforming the story and living into the future need not be overpowering experiences. No one individual is required to change the whole world. Each person of faith who chooses to work toward a hope-filled future is called to participate in communities of faith where

1. Transformation is both social and personal and is required of all who seek to journey in faith.
2. Demons are named, and people learn to speak and hear the truth.
3. Idols are confronted, as human beings, in community, seek to walk paths of fidelity to the Creator God.
4. Connections are always being sought and made more visible as persons recognize and affirm the interrelationships of all life and of all creation.
5. Compartmentalized thinking and individualistic approaches to life are rejected as incompatible with living toward the reign and realm of God.

Seeking Justice: Being Transformed

If you are neutral in a situation of injustice, you have chosen the side of the oppressor. If an elephant has his foot on the tail of the mouse, and you say you are neutral, the mouse will not appreciate your neutrality [Desmond Tutu, bishop of the Church of the Province of South Africa, quoted in Brown, 1984, p. 19].

It becomes increasingly clear that altruism cannot be the motivation for communities of faith as they seek to transform and be transformed toward a more just global village. Instead, motivation "must come from a deep personal interiority and the experience of a compassionate community." That sense of connectedness with all of creation will lead to "the dawning realization that the person I have thought of as 'other'—the stranger, the alien, the outsider—is my brother, my sister, my self" (Moran, 1989, p. 155). As Harris asserts, "The me is you, the we is us, the other is myself" (1989b, p. 130).

Journeying toward justice requires persons and communities to recognize that a heightened awareness of the larger contexts in which we live becomes crucial as we seek to understand and examine our assumptions and to expand our horizons. Being persons of faith who seek to embody justice requires compassion, caring, and commitment.

Educating for justice has generally taken one of two forms. Monette has identified them as liberal education and radical education. Liberal education has traditionally been developed and supported by clergy and professional religious educators; it uses adaptation and experience to renew existing structures. Radical education has arisen from base communities where laity in oppressed circumstances have been primary movers. It seeks to transform and advocates an interdependent way of being faithful to produce justice and major systemic change (see Monette, 1983). Both models of educating for justice can prove useful, especially if there can be authentic communication among all who seek to work toward a more just world.

Persons who live and work and have been educated in affluent cultures must acknowledge the power that their dominant culture has had in shaping the lenses through which they view life, faith, and the world. We must "separate ourselves from the dominant culture" and recognize that these are not "normal times" if we choose to commit ourselves to work toward the reign and realm of God on earth (Nelson-Pallmeyer, 1989, p. 82).

Educating for justice requires persons of faith to "combine self-acceptance with social responsibility, inner freedom with a hunger and thirst for righteousness" and to reconcile ministry with the assurance that God's love is purposeful and creative and will ultimately prevail (Wren, 1977, pp. 115-118). It requires us to reject methods of education that are hierarchical and to search for those that foster equality (which grows out of mutual respect) and participation. Concrete actions must result from educating for justice. Power is generated through dialogue, as people see and then work together toward a just and agape-motivated world (Butkus, 1983, pp. 154-155).

For the Israelites in the Hebrew Bible and for Christians, the Kingdom of God is a primary symbol of "God's everlasting and complete dominion over all creation"—which is "a Kingdom of peace and justice, wholeness and completion, happiness and freedom" (Groome, 1980, pp. 36-38). It is both present and future, and those who choose to live in covenant relationship with the Creator God become instruments of both the "challenge (denunciation) and consolation (annunciation)" of that reality (Butkus, 1983, p. 153). To journey toward justice is to join with the prophets in both speaking and living words of judgment and hope.

The search for justice and transformation—both societal and personal—are integrally interrelated. Journeying in faith is an invitation

1. To acknowledge and then seek (continuously) to remove the contextual blinders that block out parts of the world.
2. To seek to move outside the dominant culture and to recognize that for God earth has no boundaries.
3. To empathize and embody compassionate caring for all persons and for the entire creation.
4. To participate with others in ways that foster mutual respect and that call for shared responsibility—even when those others do not always do things *our* way.
5. To speak the truth as we understand it in ways that reflect both God's judgment and hope.

EIGHT

Creating Programs in Communities of Faith

To educate is not so much to teach as it is to become committed to a reality in and with people, it is to learn to live,
to encourage creativity in ourselves and others; and under
God and [God's] power, to liberate [humanity] from the
binds that pervert the development of God's image.
—*from the Work Book for the Fifth Assembly of the World
Council of Churches, quoted by Russell, 1979, p. 84*

Being Purposeful About Our Future

Mary Boys maintains that religious educators are charged with the
responsibility of making faith traditions accessible and offering
vehicles for transformation through three symbiotic modes: proclamation, narration, and interpretation. There are many methods by
which persons can be invited to proclaim, narrate, and interpret—
using body, mind, imagination, and spirit. Those who would engage in religious education have the responsibility of reflecting "the
complexity, ambiguity and mystery of the relationship of divine
and human" (1979, pp. 28–30).

It is obvious that this is not a simple task, which can be
relegated to any single means or program or staff member. It requires instead a purposeful, comprehensive plan to involve all

members of the faith community in multiple ways of hearing, assessing, sharing, celebrating, reforming, and acting as persons of faith.

This purposeful, comprehensive ministry encompasses the whole life of the faith community. It requires the ability to focus, to be assertive, and to make decisions that support the worshiping, preaching, teaching, witnessing, serving life of the community (Whitehead and Whitehead, 1980, pp. 177-180). Focusing requires listening and other interpersonal skills; it necessitates involving persons in experiential acting-reflecting-imagining activities. Assertiveness entails providing opportunities to share the stories, traditions, values, beliefs and life-styles of the faith community so that adults can enter into dialogue with others about what is proclaimed. Faithful decision making results when people in community have entered into an honest evaluation process, have been able to reach consensus, and choose to act.

Purposeful development of educational ministries necessitates discovering the interconnectedness of life's agendas as we hold in tension our commitments to the story, to our community of faith, and to society as we attempt to be ever more inclusive and global in our understanding and acting (Schipani, 1984, p. 118). It requires a recognition of the flowing stream of past, present, and future. Instrumental learning focusing on "how to" (which is often equated with all of adult learning) becomes only one form among many (Brookfield, 1986, p. 213).

Program Planning in Communities of Faith

Effective planning begins with the leader developing a plan for planning. Namely, scheduling the planning process. . . . The religious education team is responsible for planning in the following areas: organization, grouping of learners, space assignments for the learning groups, curriculum goals and materials, the teaching process, numerical growth, staffing, communication, budgeting, and meetings [Sparkman, 1989, p. 137].

In order to help persons discover a grounding in scripture and tradition, they must have access to their faith language (that is, theological language). Both Osmer (1990) and Moran (1989) emphasize the necessity for people to be fluent in their language of faith; the need for the language behind the wall must not be underestimated. Program planners must actively motivate people to grow in their ability to use the language of faith to talk about their faith journeys; there is motivation to learn this language when human beings find in their faith communities "a place of personal friendships" where they expect to experience encounters with God as they acknowledge that they are working toward "a shared enterprise of value" that "is greater than they are" (Morgan, 1986, p. 112). A myriad of ways of helping persons learn and use their faith language as they talk about real life concerns needs to be incorporated in the faith community's educational ministry.

The task of those who assume responsibility for planning educational ministries is to provide enough *continuity* to ensure survival of all that is valued by and valuable to the community of faith and enough *change* to ensure relevance. From *tradition,* as we have seen, comes a way of being and knowing that draws on the past in order to find meaning in the present and to envision a future that is filled with promise for creation, justice, and peace. Jenkins (1990, p. 221) speaks of "faithful acceptance," "faithful testing and questing," and "eventual faithful bearing witness" in helpful ways that highlight the processes of hearing and questioning, of searching and reforming, of celebrating and serving, of critiquing and imagining.

Nelson asserts that congregational life must become both the locus and the strategy for educational ministry in our secular age. This comprehensive strategy incorporates many different settings and methodologies; it recognizes that teaching and learning are being embodied in every aspect of the community's life (1989, pp. 182–230).

There are a variety of choices that offer blueprints for educational planning. Monette (1982) identifies three common, though insufficient, starting points: (1) taking a program that worked in another place and offering it in a different setting; (2) assessing the resources that are available and designing a program around those resources; and (3) taking a program offered by regional or national agencies of one's faith tradition or by some independent provider of prefabricated programs.

Key factors to consider in any program-planning process include (1) having clearly stated objectives; (2) taking into account learner preferences and abilities; (3) offering alternative materials so learners have some choices about both what and how they learn; (4) finding ways of presenting relevant content through a variety of resources; (5) referring repeatedly to the objectives so that if the discussion moves in other directions the group is able to make a conscious choice about whether objectives need to be revised or the group needs to alter its process; (6) providing feedback and review times for what has been said and done; (7) involving learners both in the planning process and as active learner participants in the teaching-learning setting; (8) building in ways of engaging in action and reflection so that opportunities to apply what is being learned are an integral part of the process (Knox, 1986, pp. 124–125).

There are at least three approaches to helping adults learn (see Knox, 1986, pp. 77–106). *Instruction* is the primary focus of the schooling models we considered in Chapter Four. Instruction can occur in many different settings. It can include programmed learning for individuals (for example, Bible study guides for individual study), small groups (book studies, topic studies), and large groups (film series, lectures). Devising an appropriate sequence becomes important as persons planning for teaching and learning through instruction consider (1) selecting topics of interest; (2) offering an overview of the journey; (3) seeking to build on existing abilities and interests and work toward mastery of essential skills and knowledge; (4) choosing activities that are related to the objective(s); (5) providing opportunities to use what is being learned; and (6) making connections and creating continuity with past learning and future goals.

Inquiry is a teaching-learning mode that is to be found in models growing out of all four of the metaphors we discussed earlier but seems particularly central to the pilgrimage and new earth metaphors. As people "walk the walk" or commit themselves to radical personal and social transformation, a wide variety of methods that require problem solving, creative imagination, and conceptual innovation are needed. Brainstorming sessions, task forces, and individual and small-group exploration are called for.

Participation is the third teaching-learning mode available to program planners. It is used primarily for models growing out of the household of faith metaphor, though it offers much to all models. Active reflection about the community's life together, as well as participation in simulations, field trips, and a variety of learning-by-doing methods, offers ways of including participatory learning in program planning.

Resources for Living and Learning Together

Now is the time to refocus our thinking from programmatic approaches to religious education and to think about resources and ways we can "fashion a people" as we seek to share our journeys with others in our own communities of faith. Maria Harris (1989b) makes a compelling case for thinking about education as artistry that is creative form. Vocation becomes central as persons live and learn, witness and serve, worship and play as faithful pilgrims along paths of faith.

When we think about curriculum, we need to consider the problems posed by both a hidden curriculum and a null curriculum. The *hidden curriculum* is those things we teach implicitly. For example, while not saying so, we may convey that our interpretation of scripture is the only true one. Or through our attitudes and interactions (or lack of interactions) toward other individuals or groups, we may convey the sense that we and those like us are superior human beings. The hidden curriculum can be very powerful and dangerous because it often is passed on and remains at a subconscious level—which means it is not subject to critical scrutiny. A *null curriculum* is that which is absent. We need to ask ourselves, "What questions, ideas, options are not being raised for consideration?" "Whose viewpoints and feelings are being ignored?" "What ways of seeing are being excluded from consideration?" Considering these questions will help us make conceptual breakthroughs and move us toward a more inclusive approach to teaching and learning.

We must no longer think of curriculum as printed resources.

Curriculum is, literally, a *course to be run* and includes the total life of the community of faith as it teaches and proclaims, worships and breaks bread, and witnesses and serves in the world. Curriculum is embedded in a particular context and is complex and multifaceted; it becomes a tool for reshaping the quality and nature of the life of the community of faith. Curriculum is all those resources and opportunities with which we can work to enhance and strengthen our journeys and our faith communities.

Curricular needs of faith communities can be seen in light of Brueggemann's canonical categories (refer to Chapter One). Curriculum must be grounded in the Word and its proclamation. Harris urges educators "to cultivate the receptivity and responsiveness that characterize genuine listening" (1989b, p. 137) as they engage in *priestly listening*—encountering the story that provides the heart of the Torah. This listening is the affirmation that makes one a part of a given faith community and tradition. It is knowing who and whose we are. But it must be balanced by *prophetic speech,* which challenges faith communities and individuals to be open to and work toward justice. Resources and strategies that will move us toward conceptual innovation and reframing are necessary curricular components. *Political advocacy* relates to the questioning, searching, decision making, and acting that is inherent in the wisdom literature as Brueggemann describes it. Curricular tools that inform and challenge, aid in reforming and renewing, and call human beings toward involvement in the world are vitally important. As Forester points out, it is through communal processes that include reviewing and critiquing, adopting parts and rejecting others, modifying and adapting, that communities learn to make sense together (1989).

Harris suggests that *inclusion, leadership,* and *outreach* are curricular tasks for faith communities (see 1989b, pp. 80–85). We must begin to name the places we choose to travel on our journeys— for example, toward more loving relationships in our families, toward greater equality in our places of work and our world, toward a spirituality where balance and mutuality are sought. Then we need to find maps for the journey and the provisions we need to sustain us as we journey toward our destinations. Curriculum resources are those necessary maps and provisions. They are clearly means rather than ends. The point is not to study a particular book or topic; rather, we should examine books and topics that suggest paths and offer food for the journey.

Worship and preaching, agendas for committees and boards, mission and outreach projects, adult-education classes, prayer and sharing groups, media, books and print resources, friends and peers are all potential curricular resources for persons embarked on journeys of and toward faith. There are many resources outside our faith communities as well. Public libraries, schools at all levels, private and governmental agencies, and other faith communities all offer rich curricular resources (human, programmatic, and material) that can enhance our teaching and learning ministries (Knox, 1986, pp. 202–217).

Needs Assessment and Evaluation as Tools for Planning

As we have seen, adults generally prefer to be active participants in the teaching and learning process rather than "recipients of education" (Knox, 1986, p. 35). They respond to methods of growing and learning that are relevant to their present and help them move toward where they hope to be. Sometimes the assumptions pastors and religious educators make about the adults in our faith communities are false. One task of assessment is to discover the preferences and perceived needs of adult members and to seek to validate or refute our assumptions.

Needs assessment needs to go hand in hand with resource evaluation. One of the real strengths of the Shepherd's Center approach to program planning (see Vogel, 1984, pp. 145–151) is that it recognizes the value of matching people's needs with the talents that those same persons have to bring to teaching-learning-serving experiences. The Shepherd's Center, founded in Kansas City but now in many locations, is an ecumenical model (Protestant, Roman Catholic, and Jewish), providing a comprehensive program for older adults in the community in order to support them in remaining as independent as possible. The model calls for examining needs under four categories: *life maintenance* (for example, health care, nutrition, transportation, and housing); *life enrichment* (current events, mission study, defensive driving, and art and music appreciation, as well as creation); *life reconstruction* (dealing with chronic illness, loss through death of spouse, retirement, and relocation); and *life transcendence* (struggling with nourishing the soul and the meaning of life and death).

These categories work as well for young adults and middle-aged persons who may be experiencing stress from both their adolescent or young adult children and their aging parents. The faith community does not have to provide ways to meet all of these needs; but because the community is concerned with people's general well-being, it is responsible for ensuring that these needs are all being satisfied. This responsibility invites us to know our local communities better and to engage in cooperative living and learning.

We will do well to heed Abraham Maslow's insight (1970, p. 92) that persons who are grappling with basic problems may not have much energy to invest in developing self-esteem and -fulfillment. Howard McClusky suggests that people must meet *coping needs* in order to address *expressive needs*. Individuals are then able to put energy into *contributive needs* (related to Erikson's need for generativity); *influence needs* are satisfied as persons find ways of affecting the larger society. Finally, *transcendence needs* call for energy and commitment (McClusky, 1976, pp. 324–355).

Planning and evaluation must be done in a broad context that invites planners and participants to examine assumptions and goals on a constant basis as well as to assess how the process and content are aiding people and groups in journeying toward their goals. An interactive, participatory approach to evaluation that considers context, content, strategies, and methodologies must be followed.

David Peterson (1983, pp. 281–282) offers three key components essential to quality evaluation. (1) When we are able to identify the needs of learners clearly, (2) when our objectives are clearly stated and are measurable, and (3) when we are able to determine that our goals have been achieved or resolved, it becomes possible to use evaluation effectively in future planning.

This is not to suggest that all goals will be specific, attainable, and measurable. For human beings who are seeking to journey in faith, things are not always clear cut. We must recognize that many of our objectives will be aimed at affective and relational growth. Nevertheless, it is generally possible to discern (if not to measure) when the "fruits of the spirit" are present and being shared.

It is vitally important that we ask the right questions. For example, we could conduct a thorough evaluative process at the conclusion of a study group that focused on what persons had learned (content) and how they had applied what they learned; at the same time—because we had not been clear that there are desired affective and relational goals as well—we might overlook the fact that several group members who were struggling with unresolved grief over the loss of spouses experienced acceptance and hope and a new sense of self that enabled them to begin living life more fully.

Evaluation of any given program must be done in light of the self-image and vision of the faith community. We need to find ways of assigning priorities and weighing the relative significance of the various outcomes we are seeking to evaluate. Consider, for example, how you would evaluate this group.

A task group was formed out of a faith community to serve as the work crew to build a house for Habitat for Humanity in a local neighborhood. The group's goals included (1) to engage in community outreach and to make a witness to the religiously un-affiliated in the neighborhood, (2) to complete this mission project on behalf of its congregation, and (3) to foster and build community within the group and congregation.

The task force worked together for over a year and became quite a close group. The house was to be blessed, and a young mother with four children would begin moving in soon. The children had begun coming to Sunday school and felt accepted and at home. During the course of the year, a homosexual member of the task force discovered that he had AIDS. Two members of the group told him that the disease was "God's judgment" and that if he did not repent, he would "go to hell." They refused to work whenever he was present. Other members of the group warmly supported the young man and began criticizing the two who rejected him to other members of the congregation. There was now a small but vocal faction in the church that was demanding that the church clearly condemn homosexuality and make clear that only through repentance could homosexuals be reconciled to God. There were others who were urging that the church begin study toward becoming a reconciling or welcoming congregation. The majority just wanted the conflict to be minimized so that there would not be a division in the community.

How would you begin an evaluative process in this case? As you contend with what it means to evaluate in order to plan and move into the future, remember that we are called to seek a holistic approach that is faithful to who and whose we are. Often there are conflicting goals and values that must to be considered. There are not simple answers, and we must try to see all sides and to create ways of turning conflict and pain into opportunities for growth.

Whatever categories you choose to use, planning processes that begin with needs and resource assessment and continue with ongoing evaluation are worth the time and energy they take (see Knox, 1986, chaps. 4 and 9, for specific approaches and guidelines). Adults who are potential participants should be involved in the planning-assessment process from the very beginning and throughout.

Journeying Toward Faithful Discipleship

Rather than concentrating on any particular model for program planning, I am proposing some principles that I believe can lead to the development of faithful models by and for particular communities of faith. These principles will be applied to the case study that was based on the Church of the Covenant's decision to become a sanctuary church.

> During the Sunday Morning Service of worship on February 12, 1984, The Church of the Covenant received Rosa, Juan and Oscar into its care. The decision by this one-thousand member Midwestern congregation to protect these three Salvadoran refugees by offering them sanctuary followed thirteen months of discernment over the scriptural meaning of hospitality in contemporary life. . . . Centerville, a community of thirty thousand, is politically conservative by its own admission. Covenant Church's membership reflects that profile. For example, in 1963 when its pastor went to Washington to march with Martin Luther King, Jr., the pastor was asked to resign. He did so. For The Church of the Covenant, therefore, to become a people of God acting on behalf of its neighbors in need, especially when these

actions conflicted with the laws of the nation, is a story as amazing as it is complex. [This book describes and analyzes] some of the dynamics of Covenant Church's journey into compassion [Slater, 1989, p. 2].

First, faith communities must hold in tension commitments (1) to conserve faithfully and transmit the faith stories, traditions, beliefs, values, and life-styles that they hold in trust; (2) to be open to the Spirit of God in the process of transforming them as they intersect with the worlds where persons live; and (3) to enable people to experience personal and communal transformation as they grow in their relationship to the Transcendent, and to become themselves transforming agents of the Transcendent as they work for justice and peace in the global community.

At the Church of the Covenant, this process began with a respected layperson's sharing his own story at an all-church, annual reflection and planning meeting. The group then encountered (anew) the gospel account of the Good Samaritan, and a lively discussion was initiated.

A short time later, a request was made of the church. Would it be willing to provide hospitality to a group from El Salvador that would be in the area speaking on behalf of the sanctuary movement? The lively discussion from the planning meeting was now brought closer to home as the session discussed this request. The ruling body of the church did not make a decision, but it did ask the missions committee to study the sanctuary movement. The process of transformative religious education had been launched.

Second, program planners must engage in conceptual blockbusting so that their existing paradigms do not hamper the creative and dynamic power of God's Spirit at work in the world and in our communities of faith.

Neither the perceived needs of learners nor faith dogmas provide adequate agendas for planning ministries of religious education. Dichotomies must give way to a growing understanding of the unity of all creation so that issues like sacred versus secular, Bible versus life, and prayer versus action no longer diverge.

At the Church of the Covenant, the missions committee became the congregation's program planners on the issue of what it would mean to become (or not to become) a sanctuary church (see Slater, 1989, pp. 4–9 for a description of the committee's deliberations). Dichotomies did give way, and conceptual breakthroughs yielded both conflict and creative energy.

Third, though responsibility for program planning may begin with a particular group within a congregation, it is ultimately the responsibility of all persons and groups within the faith community. Unless and until the missions committee (the primary initiator-educator regarding the sanctuary movement at the Church of the Covenant), the administrative body, the youth group, the staff, and individual lay persons dare to reflect on and express their questions and struggles and convictions, the educational ministry of the faith community will be less than it is called to be.

Following the missions committee's serious study, it decided in favor of the church's becoming a sanctuary church. The committee then began to plan and seek funding for a ten-week adult education course, which was held and proved to be both unifying and divisive. The missions committee then sought and received from the governing body support for creating a more broadly based and inclusive sanctuary study group.

Fourth, the faith stories and the "burning questions" of lay persons in the community of faith must be the beginning point for planning programs that will transform life and society. Involving people in honest exploration of issues that make a difference in their personal and social lives is often a slow and frustrating experience, but it can lead to deeper faith and real transformation. Hidden agendas must be unearthed, and there must be real freedom to allow programs to grow and change as boundaries move and horizons widen (or narrow, as may sometimes be the case). It is sometimes threatening to trust the Spirit of the Mysterious One to transform lives and communities, but that is what communities of seekers after Truth are called to do.

When conservative and well-respected Paul Williams (a pseudonym, as are all names in this case) spoke at the church's planning meeting and said, "I finally decided at one point that Christ might be who he said he was," people were challenged to engage in a real struggle to discover what it might mean to accept (or to reject) that faith statement. At the time that the more broadly based study group was being formed, three people (Rosa, Juan, and Oscar) arrived in Centerville from El Salvador and needed sanctuary. The study could no longer be carried on at an abstract level. The issue was now embodied in these three persons.

Fifth, an important goal of religious education is to try to see more clearly what it means to work for an active and just peace for all creation.

This objective requires overcoming any split between issues of individual and social transformation. Changed consciousness requires a holistic approach; it must reach all persons throughout their life span and cannot be focused more on children and youth than on adults in the community of faith. It reaches into every corner of persons' lives and affects all of the subcultures of which they are a part. It is both particular and universal and must not be compartmentalized.

At the Church of the Covenant, religious education was occurring in study groups and in board meetings, in informal conversations, and in the preaching and worship life of the congregation. There were serious attempts to present all sides of the issue and to provide forums where everyone had an opportunity to raise questions and to state positions.

That transformative education can occur in worship was attested to as church members reflected on what had happened with members of the national faculty seminar who contributed to Slater's book. On the Sunday preceding the meeting where the congregation would make a decision about sanctuary, the title of the associate pastor's sermon was "The Trip Back Home." He made connections between the decision the church was about to make and "the civil disobedience of the wise men, who ignored the instruction of the authorities in order to protect the life of the child, and hospitality to [sic] Jesus, Mary, and Joseph—the refugees in Egypt" (Slater, 1989, p. 17).

Once the decision to become a sanctuary church was made and hospitality was offered to Rosa, Juan, and Oscar, one member of the study group who had opposed the decision secured employment for Rosa. The life and ethos of this congregation and individuals in it took on new meanings as they embodied their faith by providing hospitality to refugees.

Sixth, openness, critical analysis, diversity, imagination, divergence, conflict, intuition, creativity, feeling, praying, and envisioning must be ingredients that are brought to activities of study and discernment in order that consensus might eventually evolve as persons seek to grow in faithful discipleship and citizenship.

Covenant Church members with many different gifts and interests were invited to work toward a new understanding of what it meant to be faithful. Many methods of learning were used—study groups, open forums, books, letters, position papers, sermons, informal conversations, personal witnessing, and personal involvement with refugees in need. Some who had not participated actively in the life of the congregation became involved—as they discovered a place where they could really make a difference and as they were encouraged to bring their questions and to use their education and skills.

Seventh, claiming one's identity within a community of faith and taking actions that bear witness to and affect the larger community involve faith communities and their individual members in making a public statement and entering into public dialogue and action.

When faith communities choose to speak and act on issues of concern to the nation and world, they are called to cooperate or compete with other institutions committed either to the status quo or to social change. At this point the language at the wall is required.

For the Chruch of the Covenant, there could be no avoiding the collision between the call to faithful discipleship (as it was coming to be heard and understood) and the law of the land. The governing body's clerk (secretary), an attorney, felt he could not in good conscience sign the church's documents informing the U.S. government of the Church of the Covenant's intention to break the law. He eventually chose to resign as clerk so that he would not have to sign the documents; however, he remained on the church's governing body and chose to live out his discipleship in other areas.

Eighth, program planning should grow out of a broad base, and it must be built on a common understanding of who and whose we are as a covenanted community of faith (that is, the community's mission statement or identity statement or covenant).

Knowing the faith story and the stories of individuals and one's own congregation provides a grounding for program planning. Linking the traditions of the past with visions for the future provides a source of energy and also serves as a compass for keeping the process on course.

Slater's case study offers ample examples of these kinds of connections. Beginning with its planning retreat, this community of faith shared its journey—its high points and its low points, its pain and its joy. Connections were also made between the journey toward becoming a sanctuary church and various community issues (for example, deciding whether or not to relocate from a downtown location) and personal concerns (deaths, vocational struggles of members involved in the sanctuary issue). These helped to create the context—what it meant to be and live in the Church of the Covenant during this time.

Ninth, program planning should reflect the educational ministry that is being planned by being egalitarian and promoting a dialogue. Planning needs to attend to the language that is used, the hidden messages that always seem to be present, and the quality of the physical and emotional environment. The quality and style of leadership and the methodologies that are employed must be in harmony with the community's core stories and traditions.

The spirit of give-and-take, the offering of pros and cons, and the depth and breadth of the study and struggle at the Church of the Covenant contributed to its ability to work through difficult and potentially divisive issues. Time taken to evaluate in order to alter future courses of action built and supported a broad base for decision making. Concern for creating consensus and reconciliation demonstrated educational ministry based on shared leadership and mutual respect. The sharing of leadership between church professionals and lay persons was crucial to the growth of this congregation.

An Invitation

People who wish to participate in program planning for educational ministry in communities of faith are invited to consider the principles I have outlined—to discuss them and to disagree with them—in order to come up with the principles that you are willing to claim as your own. Then begins the ongoing task of planning ways to journey together—exploring and questioning, praying and worshiping, studying and serving—as you seek to be guided by the call and promise of God.

Take time now to struggle and to begin to discover which ideas may guide you and those with whom you travel toward more faithful discipleship and citizenship.

NINE

Strategies
for Teaching
and Learning

To provide access means to erect bridges, to make metaphors, to build highways, to provide introductions and commentaries, to translate foreign terms, to remove barriers, to
make maps, to demolish blockages, to demonstrate effects,
to energize and sustain participation, and to be hospitable.
—Boys, 1989c, p. 209

We have seen that as persons of faith, we are asked to envision religious education in ways that force us to examine critically *all* our assumptions. Our vision should spring from a deep knowledge of the traditions and stories of our own faith community, our life within our community of faith in the present, and our future hopes for God's just rule and reign. It must also be open to and informed by the traditions and stories of other faith communities.

Joseph Gerard Brennan quotes his teacher, Alfred North Whitehead: "'There is a danger in clarity,' he would say, 'the danger of overlooking the subtleties of truth'" (1981, p. 49). It is true that people of faith must not settle for simple answers, for they cannot claim to see the whole of the picture and must therefore remain open to enlarging their canvas of life. Religious educators are called to live their lives as "parables, people who subvert, who affirm ambiguity, who are able to reconcile opposites by taking risks" (Harris, 1979, p. 51).

Religious education moves individuals beyond "critical thinking as a process . . . seen to be confined to a number of intellectual operations, such as analyzing, discriminating, integrating, and synthesizing" toward "the phenomenon of critical thinking within relationships" (Brookfield, 1987, pp. 212-214). This exercise forces us to examine context as we attempt to understand all the threats and opportunities that confront us in our day-to-day living. It requires us to open ourselves to new concepts and to aesthetic experiences that move us at the affective level in ways that release the "powers of imagination" (see Brookfield, 1987, pp. 117-131).

Teachers of adults in faith communities are called "to be a caring conduit into the experience of [their faith community] as a repenting, praying, serving community" (Dykstra, 1981, p. 129). Religious learning cannot be isolated from faithful living. Rather, it offers a safe and hospitable space in which to grapple with the contradictions that living and working in relationship with others bring. It raises issues from the larger world so that those without the resources and opportunities that are a part of the experience of many in Western faith communities may be heard and invited into the dialogue. It is within the context of vital community life that persons are challenged and supported to study, pray, and celebrate in order to live and serve faithfully in a hurting world.

A nurturing community is crucial for persons who seek to grow in faith. "Teaching is most of all," Daloz says, "a special kind of relationship, a caring stance in the moving context of our students' lives" (1986, p. 14). Harris offers the analogy of a dance that includes movement from *silence,* which flows into *remembering;* remembering leads to *ritual mourning* and the pain and grief that they entail; out of ritual mourning people join in steps of *artistry* as their creative powers are freed by naming and dealing with the exclusion, violence, and pain of their past; artistry moves them toward *new birth,* which is never free of pain but which offers fresh opportunities (1988).

Religious teachers may be seen as midwives who are present with and provide aid to those who are giving birth to the new creatures God is continually calling each of us to be. It is essential, however, to recognize that those of us who teach are *not* the primary actors in this drama. We may be the bearers of the stories and traditions and of the connecting links, but real learning happens when persons wrestle with the power of God in their own lives and strive to discern and then respond to God's call to them in their time and place.

Those who serve as midwife-teachers are available to assist others in giving birth to their own ideas, but they rarely administer anesthesia. They listen to those giving birth and seek to incubate and nourish those fragile new ideas so that they can develop in their own time and way. The focus is on the person who is giving birth and on the new life that is emerging, *not* on the wisdom and knowledge of the midwife-teacher (see Belenky, Clinchy, Goldberger, and Tarule, 1986, pp. 217–223.).

Harris wisely points out that "although the first birth *is* of the person, any pedagogy which stops at the Birthing of oneself is simply too narrow for our time. Birthing must spill over to the Birthing of just environments in society itself, for Birth and Breakthrough, as Meister Eckhart taught, are 'resurrections into justice' " (1988, p. 88). Those experiencing the pangs of new birth find themselves born into a global community where their privileges and responsibilities are integrally bound up with those of all beings in God's creation.

Storytelling is at the heart of educating for faith. Because stories have a life of their own, they offer people new ways of envisioning who and what they are called to be. Stories have no end and do not insist on simple solutions to the dilemmas that adults face.

In teaching, it is also crucial that conflict be allowed—indeed, encouraged—to surface and that the tendency to come to premature resolution of conflict be avoided. As people struggle with faith issues, they require a place and time to consider who they are, what they have done, and what God may be calling them to do. Just as Jacob wrestled with an unnamed one at Peniel (Exod. 33:22–32), so we must have our place to struggle with what it means to be in relationship with God and others.

Envisioning ways to educate in faith calls teachers to a ministry that includes

1. Identifying faith mentors, who listen and speak and live in truth.
2. Owning that ambiguity is a reality and being willing to risk responding to their own and the world's needs.
3. Engaging in the never-ending process of conceptual block-busting.
4. Becoming caring conduits who listen and affirm, challenge and prod, share stories, pray with and for others, and celebrate and break bread in community.
5. Committing ourselves to be midwife-teachers.
6. Naming and facing conflict along the way.

Principles for Teaching in Communities of Faith

> The teacher is a mediator between the knower and the known, between the learner and the subject to be learned. A teacher, not some theory, is the living link in the epistemological chain [Palmer, 1983, p. 29].

Because we generally teach as we were taught and expect to learn in a traditional fashion, it becomes a monumental task to open up new ways for adults to know and learn. The following principles foster wider horizons and more inclusiveness.

1. Teaching should be mutual, rather than hierarchical, and reflect the idea of shared leadership between church professionals and lay persons.
2. Teaching should cause people to explore and explode the boundaries that they have come to accept as given and true.
3. Teaching should emphasize relationships as well as information.
4. Teaching requires heart as well as mind.
5. Teaching should encourage imagination and creativity, as well as analysis and synthesis.
6. Teaching must foster connectedness and integration.

7. Teaching should recognize that there generally is not only one right answer.
8. Teaching must view the total life of the faith community as the agency of educational ministry.
9. Teaching should lead human beings, in community, to actions that seek justice and show loving-kindness.

The self-knowledge of those who teach in communities of faith is an important quality. It is one that enables teachers to invite learners to develop a sense of who they are and a confidence in their ability to learn; to trust and honor their own judgment and intuition; to be willing to accept their limitations and to change their positions; to be flexible in a way that respects others' opinions; to be open to facts and alternative interpretations of facts; and to be tentative and know that it is all right not "to know" (Postman and Weingartner, 1969, pp. 31–33; also see Cross, 1981; Knowles, 1984).

By fostering these qualities in learners, teachers can move toward "a sense of their personal power and self-worth" as they become able "to perceive the relative, contextual nature of previously unquestioned givens" and develop capacities "to re-create their personal and social worlds" (Brookfield, 1986, pp. 283–284).

Joyce and Weil (1986) suggest a variety of helpful models for group investigation, ways to reflect on social policy, use of simulations, and methods that may be useful to those planning comprehensive programs of adult religious education.

In an article on ideology and education, William Bean Kennedy wonders why, in spite of "better curriculum designs, materials, and support programs, the results have become less and less adequate to the needs and expectations of the religious communities" (1985, p. 331). He names the tremendous power of ideologies in shaping our world. Recognizing and naming your own demons may be one of the tasks that is required as you begin your own planning process. Kennedy suggests that other tasks may be (1) to acknowledge "the need for more aesthetic and creative modes of learning," (2) to listen attentively to the voices and experiences of those who are oppressed in our world, (3) to engage in forms of "problem-posing education," which question assumptions and offer ways of reframing questions, (4) to introduce "conflict as a tool of reflection and analysis," and (5) to encourage persons to "identify and analyze the contradictions in society" and in faith that may lead them to understand political action as a natural outgrowth of religious education.

Teachers must remain clear about the truth that those who join them are "temporary visitors" who choose to share this part of their journey with us and who accept our invitation to be in relationship for a while (Nouwen, 1986, p. 90). The language we use and the way we visualize the teacher-student relationship are significant. To talk of "pushing" students or of "my" students suggests dominance or ownership and failure to recognize the collegial nature of the experience.

Palmer urges us to keep in mind that "to teach is to create a space in which obedience to truth is practiced" (1983, p. 69). Teachers and learners take part in this process together; it is one that we never fully master in this life, so that we teachers are often learners and learners are sometimes teachers. "Practicing obedience to truth . . . is complex and confusing. We can begin only by steeping ourselves in the idea of obedience, by understanding that obedience is not a mechanical kind of truth telling but a sensitive process of feeling for the *troth* that exists between students and teachers, our subject and our world." It is a process that holds together past, present, and future, as well (Palmer, 1983, pp. 88–92).

Systems theory offers helpful insights in that it helps us focus on relationships and helps us identify "the invisible threads of influence within which any action inevitably occurs" so that we can better grasp the roles being played by teachers, learners, the subject at hand, faith stories and traditions, and the environment (Daloz, 1986, pp. 187–189). A systems approach may help us appropriate the midwife-teacher metaphor and to develop skills that lead to connectedness in teaching. This approach offers real promise for religious models of education (see Belenky, Clinchy, Goldberger, and Tarule, 1986, pp. 219–229).

There are also some very practical guidelines for those who teach. It may be surprising to discover that it is the eminent philosopher Alfred North Whitehead who says, "I lay it down as an educational axiom that in teaching you will come to grief as soon as you forget that your pupils have bodies" (1929, p. 78). No truer words have been spoken! The teacher and students need to work together to provide a comfortable physical environment that recognizes the physical and emotional needs of learners (lighting, seating, heating, ventilation, and the absence of distractions).

We must help people "escape from immersion in mass culture" in order to be able to assess it in light of the stories and values of the faith community (Brookfield, 1986, p. 137). To create an environment and design a process that promotes creative and critical thinking, we can use methods that encourage empathizing and examining issues from multiple perspectives, the development of listening skills, and the formation of networks that will provide important support and resources (see Brookfield, 1987, pp. 73–88).

Wlodkowski proposes four "cornerstones" for teachers who seek to motivate their students: "Expertise, empathy, enthusiasm, and clarity" will stand those who teach in communities of faith in good stead (see 1985, pp. 17–38). Forester's four criteria for mutual understanding are "comprehensibility, sincerity, legitimacy, and truth" (1989, p. 147).

Moran's metaphorical use of choreography to depict teaching builds on Harris's dance metaphor and offers a dynamic dimension for envisioning how these elements may interact as persons teach and learn together (1989, p. 67). To visualize expertise, empathy, enthusiasm, clarity, comprehensibility, sincerity, legitimacy, and truth as dancers and to imagine how one might join in the dance with them and with one's students suggest to me a powerful image for what it means to teach and learn together. The dance, then, creatively and imaginatively unfolds and blesses all who dare to join in it (see Harris, 1988, p. 4).

Teachers who are willing to share their true selves as they join in the dance and invite others to dance with them are the greatest gift that learners can receive. As Rogers observes, those who are able to "live constructively in this kaleidoscopically changing world" are those who choose to be learners "in a growth-promoting, facilitative, relationship with a *person*" (1969, p. 126).

A second metaphor, in addition to choreographing a dance, that may help us visualize what it means to be teacher-learners is that of a "learning conversation," which is characterized by being "reciprocal and involving" and embodying "diversity and disagreement" in serendipitous ways that bless us when we least expect it (see Brookfield, 1987, pp. 238–240). These learning conversations honor silence and the life experiences of all who take part in the conversation; they recognize that "tension can be creative" and that it is "often better to speak a question than an answer" (Palmer, 1983, pp. 81–82). The relationships that are born out of learning conversations are best nurtured by "creative, active, sensitive, accurate, empathic, non-judgmental listening" (Rogers, 1969, p. 229), coupled with an honest, open, forthright, nonjudgmental sharing of one's own self and one's deep commitments and beliefs.

The principles we describe are merely guides for the journey; the metaphors and qualities outlined here must be embodied in learners and teachers as the journey toward faith continues. Perhaps the following signposts or choreographic notes may prove helpful. Those who teach are called to be mediators, living links, creators of space; partners with those who will join in practicing obedience to truth; those who seek to make visible the invisible threads of life; those who are midwives and nurturers; storytellers and conflict-creators; keepers of silence and empathizers; sharers of knowledge and clarifiers; conversationalists, attentive listeners, speakers in truth; choreographers and dancers among the dancers; those blessed to be called teacher.

Teaching and Learning Through Studying Scripture

Before people begin to teach scripture, it is necessary for them to come to terms with what they believe about the scriptures that have grown out of and undergird their faith community. Human beings must be able to differentiate between knowing about scripture and knowing the One to whom scripture points.

One way of helping teachers clarify these ideas for themselves, as well as for learners, is for teachers to prepare a brief introduction that they might use to acquaint one good friend with another. The purpose of this exercise is twofold. It helps persons examine their own assumptions and beliefs and to be clear about how they view scripture. It lets those whom we teach know our point of view so that they are better able to evaluate what we say and to determine for themselves what they believe.

Let me illustrate. I gave the introduction below to a class I was teaching called "Teaching for Biblical Faith." When I had finished, I asked the students to take a few minutes for silent reflection and to jot down images or phrases that they would use to introduce to the group the scriptures as they know them. They then talked in small groups about their own assumptions and questions about scripture. Finally, we talked in the large group—raising questions and offering insights as we all thought together about the role scripture plays in our faith community and for each of us. Here is what I said: "Let me introduce you to the Bible as I know it. What is this book we call the Bible?"

I recently saw Topol as Tevye in *Fiddler on the Roof:*

A man for whom the "good book"—often loosely translated, but always related to daily life—was a *touchstone*, a *source* for understanding life, a *vehicle* through which God speaks to one who is attempting to make sense out of chaos

A man who never settled for easy answers; who knew that the good book says "this," but on the other hand it says "that"

A man whose relationship to God preceded and was greater than the good book, even though it played an important role; it nourished a vital relationship, where questions, anger, anguish, and hope were the order of every day

I believe that often we ask the wrong questions when we begin talking about the Bible. For me, the question is not, "Is it true?"; instead, the question is, "What is the truth that God would speak to me, us, and all through the Bible?"

For me the Bible is:

God's Living Word—which spoke to men and women of old and which speaks to me and all who will be open to hear—of the unmerited, gracious love God has for me and for all God's creation; and which makes clear the cost of discipleship

An account of God's mighty acts in history and of the response of people who have freely entered into relationship

with God and who have participated in the drama au-
thored and choreographed by God

A guide for the journey—one that comforts me when I am
afflicted and afflicts me when I am comfortable; one that
brings words of hope and judgment; one that encourages
me to grow and to see the world through eyes other than
my own

The faith community's book, written out of lived experience,
which became embodied story that was canonized by
God's people because it contained God's truth

A life-challenging, life-changing book that God's Spirit uses
to speak to me and all who read it

For me, the Bible is an invitation.

In communities of faith, it seems to me, our primary task is
to help persons encounter the living God as they seek to understand
what it is that God would have them do and be. Learning *about*
scripture may provide tools and insights, but that is not our primary
goal. Nevertheless, often scripture study seems to begin and end at
the informational level.

There are a wide range of resources available for Christian
faith communities attempting to encounter the living God through
Bible study. The work of Robin Maas (1982) and Edward Blair
(1987) are useful resources for engaging adults in historical-critical,
exegetical approaches to studying the Bible.

Wink suggests that we are at a point in history where a paradigm shift in biblical study is under way. It is a shift that does not
invalidate insights from the historical-critical method of Bible study
but that brings an openness to the sacred texts that can lead to
personal and social transformation (Wink, 1973; see also 1980). Resources for Bible study that reflect in some ways this paradigm shift
are Morrison's (1986) carefully honed questions for use in leading
group study of the gospels and Mulholland's *Shaped by the Word*
(1985). Hans-Ruedi Weber (1981) offers a global (Christian) perspective on transformative Bible study with session guides and work-
sheets. These resources involve learners at many levels—feeling,
imagination, and synthesis—as they relate Bible study to life.

Individuals and groups can see the Bible through different

cultures and perspectives in R. M. Brown (1984), Bärbel von Wartenberg-Potter (1988), John Pobee and Bärbel von Wartenberg-Potter (1986), Cain Hope Felder (1989), Renita Weems (1988), and Ernesto Cardenal (1976–1982).

There are many methodologies that can help us approach scripture in a new light. Leading groups in biblical simulations (see Miller, Snyder, and Neff, 1971, 1975) is a way of helping persons see from different perspectives and make connections as they step into the biblical world. Debriefing offers real possibilities for making significant connections between the biblical world and our own day and between persons and situations in biblical times and the conflicts and decisions that confront us in our current everyday lives.

Murray (1987) proposes many different strategies that involve the whole adult person in Bible study. His "reverse paraphrase" technique (people state the opposite of what a passage says) can be threatening but also very enlightening. He suggests ways of using pictures, drama, role playing, and all of the senses in creative and stimulating ways.

Jewish ways of studying Torah and Talmud, as illustrated in Chapter Three, also strive to involve the whole person and to encourage enountering religious truth in embodied and life-transforming ways. Resources useful in examining the Hebrew Bible include Fishbane (1979) and Levenson (1985).

These same approaches might be used to study sacred scriptures from other faith traditions, as well. The scriptures from Muslim, Buddhist, and Baha'i traditions, for example, can help Christians and Jews better understand their sisters and brothers (who are more and more often literally, as well as figuratively, our neighbors) who may journey toward the Holy One on a different road but who may enrich our own faith. Christians will grow in their own understanding when they try to read the Hebrew scriptures through the eyes of their Jewish neighbors, rather than reading Christian interpretations into Hebrew scripture. Jews may be enriched, as well, when they discover the freedom to encounter Jesus as a prophet and teacher, even though they do not accept that he is God incarnate. There must be room for alternative readings and understanding, and all will be blessed when we become able to accept that faith sharing does not have to lead to some being right and others wrong.

C. S. Lewis in his *Chronicles of Narnia* paints a wonderfully powerful picture of the all-encompassing love of an inclusive God, when a follower of Tash (who embodies evil) meets the lion, Aslan (who embodies goodness), and realizes that his whole life has been spent giving allegiance to one who opposed the lion.

> Determined to see truth and good, embodied, he dares to look Aslan in the eye and then expects to die. To his amazement, the "Glorious One bent down, touched my forehead, . . . and said, Son, thou art welcome." But being a person committed to truth as he understood it, the welcomed one said, "Alas, Lord, I am no son of Thine but the servant of Tash." Aslan answered, "Child, all the service thou hast done to Tash, I account as service to me." Unable to comprehend this gift and troubled by his memory that the Ape had claimed that Aslan and Tash were really one, he dared to ask the Lion if this were so. "The Lion growled so that the earth shook (but his wrath was not against me) and said, It is false." The truth is that no matter whose name is given allegiance, the Glorious One receives and rewards acts of faithfulness while Tash receives and punishes all who commit vile acts. Still unable to comprehend this graciousness, and still bound to speak the truth, he said once more, "I have been seeking Tash all my days." "Beloved," said the Glorious One, "unless thy desire had been for me thou wouldst not have sought so long and so truly. For all find what they truly seek" [Lewis, 1956, pp. 164–165].

Teaching and Learning
Through Questioning and Discussing

There are times when the group needs to learn the facts. When these will help the group engage in more informed exploration, there is then a place for who, what, when, and where. There are times when the group process and individual understanding will be enhanced by seeking to define, identify, and recall. Comprehension and interpretation questions ask persons to find answers and to describe, compare and contrast, interpret, and relate (Wlodkowski, 1985, pp. 164–165). Questions that encourage imaginative and creative thinking may focus on feeling, imagining, projecting, supposing, envisioning, and dreaming.

Knowles's idea that there is a progression from behaviorist theories of learning, to cognitive theories, and then toward humanistic theories recognizes the movement of adults from simple tasks to highly complex, broad ways of knowing. Being attuned to this progression is useful for those who seek to teach in communities of faith (1989, p. 48; see also 1975 and 1980; Kidd, 1973, chap. 7). As we invite persons to enter into group reflection and sharing about life-transforming issues, we should pose questions that recognize the need for each participant's investment in and responsibility for the group process. We must keep in mind the high levels of complexity of the issues and the necessity for the most complete responses as we seek to provide the framework for fruitful explorations of faith and life.

Being clear about our goals and determining what we need to know will help us choose the kinds of questions that will facilitate the group process. Adults generally want to have a part in determining the agenda and in creating a trusting and open atmosphere, where there are no unnecessary surprises and all are there because they want to be part of the agreed-upon study or task.

At the same time, there are questions that are *not* helpful to group discussion. For instance, unless people are faced with a "forced choice," which will then lead to discussion and a deeper exploration of the issue, yes-no questions generally do not serve the group well. Adults tend to resent being asked questions when the teacher knows the answer; too many adults have a history of being hesitant to answer because they fear the embarrassment of being wrong. Questions perceived as containing a "trick" are also very detrimental. Putting adults "on the spot" or embarrassing them is to be avoided at all costs. Questions that expect the group to read the teacher's mind are likely to be resented. I was once part of a continuing education course where the teacher asked, "Why do you think I chose to use this video?" None of us had the slightest idea, and he would not let go of the question. The atmosphere in that class (which was scheduled for two more two-hour sessions) was irretrievably damaged. I must confess that I skipped the last session.

Creating a safe and hospitable space where adults come to

realize that any question is valid must be a high priority for those who teach adults. People should know that if they have a question, almost certainly there are others wondering about the same thing. Teachers who freely admit (when it is true) that they do not have the answers contribute greatly to an open, searching climate.

Teachers who draw on the life experiences and wisdom of group members create a sense of mutuality that generates energy within the group. Questions are to be encouraged that value life experiences and allow for multiple answers, which, taken together, may help the group expand its understanding. Probing questions that inspire people to explain further, illustrate, and think of situations where a particular idea might not work or might be detrimental can help the group clarify its thinking.

Teachers need to be careful about making judgmental responses, which we often do in an attempt to provide positive feedback. There is a trap, however; it is disconcerting to have nothing to say when one has just responded to the last three contributions with "wonderful!" "excellent!" "very insightful!" and then a not-so-helpful comment is offered. Saying nothing becomes a loud, negative response.

As previously noted, the practice of leading discussions has often gotten a bad reputation because teachers have assumed that they need not prepare beyond reading the relevant material beforehand. It is my experience that forming good discussion questions, ones that help a group wrestle with significant issues and eventually move toward consensus or some other closure, takes a great deal of time and thought. In preparing for a class discussion, I generally formulate many more questions than I will use so that I have flexibility; I can facilitate rather than control. There are times when, not too long into the discussion, my questions become no longer relevant. But those times are rare, and even then the thought and advanced planning make me better able to be responsive to the group's new direction.

What does a skilled discussion leader do about "chasing rabbits"—that is, allowing the group to move away from its agenda to pursue tangential questions? There is not an easy answer to this problem, though it is an extremely important one to consider. Sometimes it is appropriate for the leader to assume responsibility for calling the group back to its agenda. When the leader is not sure whether the question involves a necessary "detour," the decision should be presented to the group. But I believe it is the responsibility of the leader to identify diversionary tactics and questions and to ask the group to decide if a particular tack will advance its purposes.

Finding ways to elicit differing points of view, to encourage energetic give-and-take, to allow conflict to be a creative and positive part of the process (and, therefore, not being afraid to let it run its course), and to know when it is time to suggest that sometimes we are called on "to agree to disagree" requires sensitivity to all persons in the group and considerable practice. Effective group-discussion leaders must have a strong-enough sense of self so that they do not take things "personally" and thus they do not have to defend themselves. They do not always have to have the last word. Effective leaders need skills in listening, sensing, motivating, eliciting, summarizing, challenging, naming, and dealing with persons whose manner is destructive to the group. The leader's primary commitment must be to the health of the whole group, and that sometimes requires making painful choices that may potentially alienate a group member.

My own experience is that groups that want to be spontaneous and discuss whatever is on their minds may provide significant opportunities for fellowship but not very effective forms of seeking, purposefully, to grow in faith. Groups that desire to journey together toward deeper and broader faith must have leaders who share with the whole group a sense of where they are headed and how they hope to travel.

Teaching and Learning Through the Creative Arts

We are more aware than ever that not all persons learn best by thinking and analyzing. For some, transformational growth most often results from feeling and intuition. Opportunities to experience music, art, dance, drama, and silence may be the basis of significant learning.

Harris (1989a) offers a valuable resource for persons who want to teach in this mode. Keeping a journal, dancing, molding clay, observing a plant, singing and composing, acting, and becoming both transformed and transforming agents in the world characterize this approach to adult religious education. One woman's response to learning by getting in touch with her spirit in this way challenges all who seek to grow in faith:

> The new life that is the result of this [spirituality] process is vulnerable, demanding, fragile, hungry, out-crying, dependent on other nurture for continued existence. . . . I once thought spirituality to be a privatized thing. It was what I "did" internally in an attempt to find God. Instead, all along, it was God who was seeking me, and I was refusing to come out, opting to stay in the gestating place, in the dark. . . . My spirituality has been born, and now I will seek to remain aware of my dependence on other sources for continued life, seek to allow the growth to happen, not to hinder it, seek and receive the nurture that is there for me, given through others by the Source of Life [Harris, 1989a, p. 97].

Many women are experiencing rebirth as they discover forms of learning that build on relationships and focus on being connected in holistic ways while encouraging creative expression. I know men as well who welcome this approach. I pray for the day when all persons will have opportunities to journey in a way that draws out the deepest and best of all of our affective, our cognitive, and our creative gifts—all of which make us children of God made in God's image.

Teaching and Learning Through Acting and Reflecting

A number of years ago my husband and I led a retreat for the bishop, district superintendents, and conference staff of our annual conference in the United Methodist Church. It was a stimulating and learning time for us all as we reflected on a praxis way of knowing and doing. Recently I was leading a retreat where a member of that conference staff was in attendance, and I asked him how this year's retreat had been.

There is now a two-year cycle for this retreat. They still go to a retreat center, but in alternate years they stay in Des Moines, where the conference headquarters are. Instead of "going apart," they choose to "go into the world." They still eat, study, sing, pray, and have fellowship together, but from ten to four each day they also work together, building a home with Habitat for Humanity. When they meet in the evenings to reflect and feast around the table, they may have blisters and sore backs, but they also bring increased sensitivity to the needs of the poor and dispossessed in our world and an awareness of what it means to "walk the walk, as well as to talk the talk." It seems good to me to belong to an annual conference where those to whom I am accountable choose to go into the world to serve as well as to retreat to a place set apart to reflect. All who seek to journey in faith need to find ways to engage in both of these approaches to learning.

Work camps, either near our rural or urban homes or in the furthest corners of the earth, provide opportunities for adults to engage in an action-reflection approach to religious education. Short-term projects working with troubled children and youth or with the poor elderly in one's own neighborhood or county offer ways of embodying faith.

Planning and leading these kinds of teaching-learning experiences require skills in careful advance planning, in facilitating group process, and in being attentive to timing and the creation of appropriate environments for times of working, reflecting, playing, praying, singing, celebrating, and relaxing. Teachers need flexibility and a good sense of humor! They should know how to motivate and to draw out skills group members may not know they have. Teaching requires a willingness to risk innovative (almost unimaginable) approaches when tried methods are inappropriate. The ability to find a friend among the strangers one meets and to accept people whose life-styles and beliefs may be very different from one's own has enormous value for leaders of action-reflection ways of journeying.

Keys to Educating in Faith

People's lives provide maps for journeying in faith as we discover that
          Clarity sometimes muddies the waters.

Caring embodies faithful living.
　　Communities that nurture become safe, for hospitable spaces
　　　Conceptual innovation as we begin
Choreographing dances of life that connect
　silence,
　　remembering,
　　　ritual mourning,
　　　　artistry,
　birthing, . . . that are
Calling for midwife-teachers who become
　Connecting links fostering
　　Committed living through
　　　Charismatically sharing stories of faith as we willingly
　　　become
Conflict-embracing in order to empower persons to move with truth
and integrity toward
　Consensual living as a
　　searching,
　　　growing,
　　　　Spirit-empowered
Community of faith.
Teaching and learning calls people of faith to be about
　Engaging ourselves in
　　seeing,
　　　hearing,
　　　　reflecting, and
　Embodying scripture in holistic ways that are
　　affective,
　　　cognitive,
　　　　imaginal,
　　　　volitional,
　and that involve those who journey together in
　　Exploring questions in discussions that lead to
　　　Embodying faith in all areas of living.
　　　Expressing
　　　　doubts,
　　　　　fears,
　　　　　　anger,

questions,
hopes,
dreams,
visions,
through the imaginative, creative arts and
Entering into acting and reflecting (praxis) ways of knowing and
doing that incorporate
worshiping and witnessing,
studying and serving,
praying and singing,
and sharing sacramental acts in
communities of faithful pilgrims who are
dancing,
acting,
reflecting,
working,
envisioning,
being.
Journeying toward transformation and
working toward that
all-inclusive,
justice-filled,
peace-abiding
reign and realm of the One
who is "I AM."

TEN

Supporting Journeys
of Learning
Within and Across
Communities of Faith

The charismatic authority of Jesus that enabled him to
preach, heal, and work among the people was not something he kept to himself. Thus, . . . in the story of the five
thousand we hear that he involved the disciples and the
people in the feeding (Mk. 6:30–44). In a household of freedom the charisma of God's Spirit is recognized among the
people, but those who lead find that their job description is
one of *diakonos*, servant, and the job description is to work
themselves out of a job. Charisma becomes a gift of empow-
erment for others. . . .

—Russell, 1987, p. 98

Stories, we are told, are among the most powerful ways of sharing
faith. Kaelene Arvidson-Hicks recounts this story of a powerful experience she had while serving for fifteen months in the Philippines as
a mission intern with the Board of Global Ministries (1987–1988) of
the United Methodist Church. Here is her story of the Kankana-ay
people, one of fourteen ethnolinguistic groups living in the Cordillera mountain range on the main island of Luzon in the Philippines.

Restoration! Salvation!

The time is coming when I will restore my people . . .
I will bring them back to the land that I gave their
ancestors . . . [Jer. 30:3].

Only a month after arriving in the Philippines, I received
an invitation to visit some faith communities in the high-
lands of the Cordillera mountains. I received the invitation
with anticipation and excitement.

In the dark morning hours of the following day, I
boarded a bus bulging with chickens, pigs, and supplies for
those traveling back to their remote mountain barrios. Every
nook and cranny was utilized for the precious resources of
the mountain people that would need to last until their next
trip to the city center of Baguio.

After mounting five sacks of palay (rice) and receiving an abundance of curious gazes from the native travelers,
I came to the conclusion that there were no more vacant
seats. Thankfully, several Igorot women took pity on my
ignorance. They shuffled bags of squawking chickens and
sacks of seed and pointed with the most insistent hospitality
to the portion of a seat they had made for me. Twenty others
boarded after me. There was always room for one more.

The day's challenge was ahead of us. We set out on
a treacherous gravel road with hairpin turns scanning seas
of terraced vegetables and rice. Eight hours later the dust
storm from the mountain road subsided, and the cliffed
edges ceased. I found myself in the company of another for-
eigner and two young guides.

We trudged along a path lined with arching pines.
Together—our guides with rubber "thongs" and generous
spirits, we foreigners with mountain boots and oversized
backpacks—journeyed to the destined faith community.

As we trailed through luscious expanses of green
mountain slopes and stretching pines, we gawked in utter
amazement at the ancient rice terraces carved into the mountain's side. The local Kankana-ay people had woven their
very existence into the earth's terrain. The century-old
layered terraces stood as a witness to generations of nurture
for the land as the sacred source of life and continuity to
their ancestral heritage.

"How far is it?" I asked, gleeful with the delights of
the astounding beauty. "Four to six hours na laeng," came
the reply. We teetered along paths not wider than the length
of two human feet, trembling at every bend and rocky abyss.

We hurried across foot bridges suspended over the river's gorge, which swayed at the wind's command.

Almost six hours later I asked again, "How much farther?" "Oh, it's just over this mountain," said the one I called "teacher." I stared in disbelief. "There," he emphasized, jutting his chin into the severe ascent of our path as if I were to understand exactly the distance ahead. Two days later we arrived at our destination in time for the Sunday morning worship.

Narseeso, our host, seated us between the men—at the forefront of his house; the women gathered at the edges of the circle. The young mothers clustered at the doorway, while the children peered in from the porch, releasing an occasional scatter of laughter. . . . The elder women sang a wonderful song of welcome and blessing. The worship had begun.

The translation of their song reminded me of a song we had sung to visitors in my own Sunday school class while growing up: "There's a welcome here, there's a welcome here. . . ." And as the worship unfolded, I felt oddly disappointed. I had come to encounter what I had hoped to be a distinctive way of worship of this indigenous community, yet the entire service seemed very similar to worship as I have always known it: there was scripture reading from the Gospel of John, joyful singing, fervent prayer, and a sort of dialogue sermon. Even momentary translations of the sermon seemed somehow familiar.

Then, when I thought worship was about to close, something very strange happened. One member of the group—one who had journeyed for several hours from a neighboring barrio—drew a sharp object out of his pocket. The worship proceeded with what was a tooth-pulling ceremony! The singing continued, and there was much fervent prayer.

Five persons got their teeth pulled that morning. I was aghast. But to them it was simple and obvious: there were five among them who needed their teeth pulled and one present that morning who could meet this need, so they chose to address this physical need as a part of their community worship.

Then, once again, when I thought we were finally about to close the morning worship, we were invited to join the tribal elders for discussion. During this part of the worship, the problems of the community were brought to the elders. That morning the community addressed the need to construct an irrigation system.

By way of background the elders explained to us the source of their new difficulty: "Up until now Apo Kabunian (their name for "Lord of us all") has always provided the rain we need to grow the rice on the mountain terrace," they said. "But Apo Kabunian can no longer give us the rain because the logging companies have skinned the mountain of their trees and lowered the water table."

The irresponsible logging practices have permanently damaged the natural irrigation cycle on the mountain slopes. Together the elders and the community members discussed this problem. They identified the practices of the logging companies as "sin" separating them from Apo Kabunian's blessing (salvation), and they spoke of how ecological abuse threatened their symbiotic relationship to the sacred ancestral domain, their relationship with the Creator God, and their very cultural survival as a people: "In the earth, the seas, the skies, and the fruits of the land is God's presence, God's blessing. Our soul remains tied to the land after death. Thus the ancestors are always present with the land and the people. The earth receives our souls after death and from the earth we are given our sustenance, our life, and our continuity as a people. Through the sweat of our labor we nourish the land, the hope for our children's future. And through the tears of our anguish we struggle to be able to care for the ancestral domain. For if we do not care for the earth, we affront Apo Kabunian and the spirits of our ancestors."

As I reflected on their testimony, it became obvious to me that for the indigenous communities of the Cordillera, the land and its produce were not economic assets but expressions of God's love and blessing. Their nurture of the land with their sweat and tears is a deeply spiritual responsibility, and their struggle to keep and care for the ancestral domain is a spiritual struggle integrally tied to the promises of salvation.

In no other time in my life has the interconnectedness of God's spiritual and material salvation been so real. I experienced that morning a community that had come together out of a spiritual need to be community. As they gathered, they addressed the physical needs of the community in their midst, and they encountered their collective call to struggle against the sin that threatens their relationship to the sacred ancestral domain, Creator God—life itself.

Worship that morning did indeed end. It ended with joyful song, fervent prayer, and the sharing of rice and wine. But in another way the worship which I had thought had ended was also continuing. Worship today is continuing, and God's struggle for salvation in all its fullness is continuing.

Before sharing the rice wine, Apo Narseeso held up the large pottery jar in his hands and prayed, "Apo Kabunian, grant us the strength to work and live so that our children will inherit that which You have given and what we justly have worked for."

Apo Narseeso's prayer was a cry to restore the very covenant God gave to the tribes of Israel through their ancient ancestor in faith, Abraham (Gen. 12:1).

Restoration of the Cordillera people to the full rights of their ancestral domain is recognition of their right to sustain themselves, maintain their cultural identity, and receive the full blessings of Creator God, Apo Kabunian.

The prophet Jeremiah echoed the promise of the covenant to the tribes of Israel who, centuries after Abraham, were stripped of their land and their self-rule and dominated by a foreign power:

In benediction:

The struggle for the land and care of the ancestral domain is a spiritual struggle intimately bound to the promises of salvation. Restoration of the Cordillera people to the full rights of their ancestral domain and its development is recognition of their right to sustain themselves, maintain their cultural identity, and receive the full blessings of Creator God, Apo Kabunian.

As heirs to the Abrahamic covenant, we also, together with the indigenous peoples of the Philippines and throughout the world, are entrusted with the care and cultivation of the earth, the restoration of a people to their rightful inheritance, and the full blessings of Creator God, Apo Kabunian [Kaelene Arvidson-Hicks].

Making Connections

I am grateful to Kaelene for contributing her story. It is the embodiment of one journey—a journey that began at her birth and was focused by her decision to become a short-term mission intern; that led her onto that crowded bus; that helped her to her destination, where she experienced hospitality, and shared stories and traditions; that provided the opportunity to reflect and seek to understand, pray, sing, hear the Word, share rice and wine at table, and decide that ways to act were all a part of her sharing this faith community's story. Her journey then led her back to communities of faith at home in the United States where she continues to share and grow.

As this book has evolved, I have become increasingly convinced that the key to adult religious education is to be found in *making connections*—within our own selves, with persons in our own faith communities, among laity and professional church staff, between professional educators and pastors, with those in our own and other Christian traditions, between Christians and Jews, with persons of other faith traditions (both Eastern and Western world religions and the religions of indigenous peoples), and with all persons of good will who are committed to working toward a world that is justice-producing and life-sustaining for the planet and every being on it.

Sculpting meaning and nourishing souls have much to do with forming connections. Examples of a serious lack of connections can be found now in the United States, where many people seem to make political and religious decisions on the basis of a *single* issue. To support or reject a political candidate or to choose to leave a particular faith community on the basis of its position on one issue (be it abortion, homosexuality, gun control, or whatever) reflects a kind of compartmentalized thinking that is destructive to the human community and may lead to the destruction of the planet.

Connections at all of the levels suggested above are best made through direct, shared experiences. They become increasingly important as our society grows more and more pluralistic. "A Christian cannot completely understand, for example, what it is to be a Jew unless he or she has had the experience of encountering a member of the tradition, of internalizing the person's personal faith journey, and of appreciating the role of the religion in times of suffering. Part of the function of religion cross-culturally is to help explain, justify, and interpret the meaning of suffering. This dimension is never just an abstraction but is always of the most intimate and personal nature. To understand this function through the medium of experience helps to reduce the effect of stereotypes based on culture or religion" (Richardson, 1988, p. 200).

Let me illustrate. Several years ago I was a member of a women's support group, which included three Sisters of St. Francis, one Sister of Charity, and me—a United Methodist diaconal minister of education. That group was a place for open sharing and honest naming of both pains and joys. Several of the women had become friends with Magda Herzberger, a woman who was separated from her parents at age eighteen and survived Auschwitz, where she hauled "charred remains of innocent victims from the belching furnaces where the gassed bodies were destroyed," and then Bremen and Bergen-Belsen until she weighed only seventy-five pounds and was too weak to work anymore. After two failed attempts to escape, she resigned herself to death and lay down to die; she was awakened by a British soldier announcing that they had liberated Bergen-Belsen. Her father was killed at Dachau, and it was eighteen months before she was reunited with her mother, who had also survived Auschwitz. Magda invited our group to attend her synagogue's service of remembrance of the holocaust. Several weeks later she and her aged mother joined us at dinner; she talked of her experiences and read some of her poetry to us. Perhaps you can picture us as we listened to Magda.

Sabbath Lights
(to my Mother)

Every Friday night
My mother would pray
By the candlelight. . . .
I remember her slim figure;
Her shiny black hair
Was lightly covered
With a dainty lace;
She wore a happy smile
On her pretty face.
In a soft voice,
With closed eyes,
She uttered slowly
Her words of benediction:
    Blessed art Thou,
    O, Lord, our God,
    King of the Universe,
    Who has sanctified us
    By Thy laws
    And commanded us
    To kindle
    The Sabbath light
Then, she kissed me,
And my father,
With affection—
I saw the white bread
And the red wine

On the table.
The plates, the glasses,
And the silverware
Were neatly spread
On the handstitched cloth.
I looked at my parents,
Feeling such a deep love for both.
I was only seventeen years old,
But I knew by then
That love is more precious
Than diamonds or gold.

I saw my mother
Two years later . . .
Still lighting the candles
Each Friday night.
But tears and sorrow
Shadowed our weekly ritual—
We'd learned my father had died
During his captivity
In the extermination camps
Of Germany.

And now, so many years later,
I have a family of my own
With children who are fully grown.
My mother still lights
The candles in her home,
    But she is all alone. . . .

Prayer

Almighty God,
Upon you I call.
Don't let evil spirits
Possess my soul—
Don't let hatred
Strangle my love,
Or despair
Crush my hope—
Tie me with the rope
Of patience
To the pillar of strength
When anger erupts
In my mind—
Don't let emotion
Blind my reason—

> Teach me the psalm
> Of faith
> And restore my calm—
> Dispel my doubts and fears
> While the bells of life
> Toll my years—
> Let the warm rays
> Of affection and compassion
> Conquer my spirit—
> O, Lord, our God
> Please disperse
> The seeds of peace
> And brotherhood
> Upon the earth,
> As time rolls
> On the wheels
> Of the universe—
>   [Herzberger, 1983, pp. 71–72 and 111–112]

As we ate together, sang, listened, prayed, and cried, connections were made that go far beyond the cognitive and link us in profound ways. Adult religious education needs to offer this kind of experience.

Richardson suggests that in this diverse age, there is a need for "mediating institutions," which can provide a secure and hospitable space where public and private, those who are like us and those who are different, can meet. These institutions may be able to help our societies move away from schizophrenic compartmentalization, which is so destructive to both individuals and communities. Schools and ecumenical or cross-cultural organizations might serve as mediating institutions and provide forums where people are able to listen and speak, raise questions of identity, and attempt to explain and understand one another's beliefs and lifestyles. Providing a place where persons from differing faith traditions can begin to make sense, make connections, and feed souls is a vital function that ecumenical communities may be able to serve (Richardson, 1988, p. 202).

Individual communities of faith can also become active as mediating institutions when they invite others to come and share. One congregation I have been a part of has a tradition of offering as a gift to the community a discussion-lecture series that brings in renowned speakers (for example, Pulitzer-Prize winners). Being hospitable requires remembering and respecting the traditions of those one invites. I remember one Jewish woman commenting that she had really enjoyed the lecture and discussion; however, the most impressive thing to her was that the hospitality committee served kosher cookies! There must be an openness to share and a willingness to honor as equals those who are invited to the table.

On the other hand, I was once part of a denominational effort by two different boards to engage in a cooperative book publication project exploring a variety of forms of ministry. When it got to the "bottom line," one group was not willing to accept what the second group needed to say about its own form of ministry. When the second group sought to discuss why what it wanted to say was crucial to its self-understanding and was theologically accurate, the first group replied, "We're paying for this book, and you can't say it that way!" Any institution (or person) that under duress will "pull rank" cannot become a mediating institution (person).

Mediation—a form of making connections—offers ways of bringing together diverse individuals and groups so that they are able to understand and reflect on one another's experiences. It becomes possible to find pathways, different from those of pluralism or assimilation, toward understanding that may (if all choose to make a commitment) lead to a consensus-building process. At the very least, mediation can promote more clarity about who persons and groups are and what they really believe; it can provide opportunities to work jointly toward mutual goals. Finally, mediating groups may be able to build bridges between and among differing communities of faith and various national and ethnic groups; they can begin to build relationships and aid persons and groups in making connections "between the pluralistic private world and the more homogeneous realm of public life" (Richardson, 1988, pp. 219–220).

Indeed, some maintain that it is through sacramental imagination that connections might most fruitfully be made as individuals and communities seek to work systemically toward the reign and realm of God (Seymour, O'Gorman, and Foster, 1984, p. 151). The incarnation provides a powerful metaphor for Christians who seek to grasp what it means to accept the role of mediator and to offer sacrificial love without condition.

It may be time to take seriously the words of George Albert Coe: "Gladly co-operating with every one who endeavors to put the love of one's neighbor into education, we shall go on to probe the educational significance of the two great commandments in the Christian faith. For us there must be a theory and a practice in which the love of God to us and our love to [God] are not separated from, but realized in, our efforts toward ideal society, the family or kingdom of God" (1917, p. 9).

Sharing Power: Trading Ladders for Lattices

Our world is calling for—indeed, its future depends on—an immense shift that makes a global perspective part of our personal and communal and national and international relationships. This concept became more imaginable and was filled with new meaning once astronauts had viewed the earth from outer space and brought back pictures; they move us because of their incredible beauty and at the same time remind us that we are infinitely small and that our world is fragile. It is not easy to move in a few decades from an emerging glimpse of what it means to develop a global perspective, to claiming it as a dominant, life-transforming metaphor. Yet the rapidity of change and the threats to the planet are so great that it seems our only option.

What does a global perspective require? We people of faith in the more affluent nations must carefully examine the lenses through which we see the world in order to identify how they are skewing our vision. Emerging Korean minjung theologians tell us that we must "de-Europeanize" Christianity, while a Brazilian theologian calls for its "de-Northification." Christians must address the question, "What does the gospel look like when it's been unwrapped from its northern, European shell and allowed to take root and flower in a quite other culture?" (Cox, 1988b, p. 110).

Yet can we even comprehend what this requires of us when we cannot get even our own houses in order? I have spent much energy working with church staffs in conflict. We must invest the time and energy necessary to break down the ladders (hierarchies) that sap our energy and make a travesty of our ministries—ladders that place women on one rung and men on another, professional educators on one rung and ordained clergy on another, laity on lower rungs than professional church staff, support staff on perhaps the lowest rungs of all. Unless and until we are willing to throw out our ladders and to replace them with lattices—where there are many ways to journey in faith and equally fine places to bloom exist all over the lattice and where the health of the whole plant is dependent on the well-being of every leaf and every blossom and all are connected to God, the root—faith communities will not be able to bear their own weight.

If we identify and honestly confront the pain and promise that minority persons and faith communities experience, they will be helped to find their voices and we to hear with empathy. Churches and synagogues (and other faith communities) will then be able to be liberated from the sins of oppression that have for too long marred our witness to the life-giving, all-embracing love of God (see Matsuoka, 1990).

Adult religious education must be seen as a vital strategy for faith communities, as laity, clergy, and professional educators together recognize that being disciples is a lifelong journey toward truth in community. For Christians this recognition calls us to study, worship, and enjoy fellowship; to baptize and gather around the table; and to scatter to witness and serve as we become the body of Christ in the world. Those who are gifted and called to teach must learn and relearn stories and traditions from the faith community throughout time and around the world and must discover resources for the journey.

Such religious education must look long and hard at ways in which the dominant culture (whether it is clerical, patriarchal, classist, North American, or Christian) is so often uncritically accepted. Our rigidity causes us to miss the talents and challenges that culturally and ethnically diverse communities, laity, the poor, and all who are outside the dominant power structure offer us. Our standard operating procedures must be replaced so that there are new arenas for dialogue that invite alternative ways of knowing that respect and honor the worth, dignity, and right of everyone to participate. In this way communities may begin to nurture and build a global community of this broken and threatened world (Matsuoka, 1990, pp. 117–118).

Those who choose a Christian path for their life journey (and there are certainly other viable paths, as well) may be strengthened by the image of God's "homecoming banquet where all the children of earth, including the least of our sisters and brothers and even you and me, will sit at table in the mother-father's house." Home can be for us "a circle that erupted at Pentecost to include people of every nation on earth" (Raines, 1984, p. 152).

Before we can sit at the final banquet table, we are called to be "advocates of all human life" (Cox, 1983, p. 145). The religious education to which we commit ourselves must open itself to the need for "conversion away from sin, personal-and-social," so that we are compelled to identify with "the poor, the dispossessed, the disfavored and with the movements toward their emancipation, an identification that precedes the critical reflection on policy and strategy" (Baum, 1975, p. 220). As Jenkins asserts: "I am bound to bear witness to you that God is God—the living God who is active today to smash all the idols of religion in which we seek to shut God up, and active today to meet and fulfil all the needs and possibilities of truly human living, in this world and beyond it" (1990, p. 14).

Moving Toward Dialogue with Other Faiths

> From Judaism, Christianity, and Islam to Hinduism, Buddhism, Taoism, and Native American and Goddess religions, each offers images of the sacred web into which we are woven [Joanna Macy, quoted in Fox, 1988, p. 159].

"If Jews, Christians, and Muslims lived respectively on Mars, Venus, and Mercury, there would be little problem," Moran observes. "But can all three live in Jerusalem or in Brooklyn?" (1989, p. 26). The answer, of course, is that they do—along with persons from all the other faiths mentioned by Macy and more besides. They also all live in my home of Chicago and in many other cities and towns around the world. There is a Buddhist Sunday school in a neighboring community, and Muslims, Jews, and Christians live on my block.

The survival of the Christian faith (in affluent nations at least) depends in some measure on how we recognize and respond to "a profound shift in the areas where Christianity is growing today—a shift from north to south, from west to east—that is, away from the so-called first world. By the year 2000, more Christians will be living outside than within the confines of the old Western Christendom" (May, 1990, p. 38). Add to this the fact that by the year 2000 no more than 16 percent of the world's population are expected to be Christian (Song, 1990, p. 176).

Song seems right to assert that "to make a clean break with other religions is no longer a viable option for Christians. Demographically, it is impossible. Socially and politically, it is an illusion. Religiously, it is sheer arrogance. . . . Theologically [it] is not a viable position either. God, for one thing, is not the God of Christians alone. God is the God of all humanity. This is what we Christians profess. How can we, then, exclude God from working among other people in different ways, even in ways not compatible with what we believe and the way we live as Christians?" (1990, p. 176).

Not only does the world demand of us a more open stance and a willingness to engage in dialogue in creative and imaginative ways, but our desire to remain in touch with our own children and the young people who have grown up in our churches necessitates that we become more knowledgeable about and interested in the religious traditions that they are exploring in increasing numbers (Parks, 1986, pp. 203–204). Cox believes that many seekers who are turning to Eastern religions "are searching for a discipline that will enable them to meet both the sacred and the secular aspects of life with a directness not gutted by abstraction or sullied by analysis. . . . It is a search for an unaffected and honest encounter with all one meets—with nature, other people and the self" (1988b, pp. 80–81).

Now is the time to learn how to participate in interfaith dialogue that does not seek to judge or convert others; nor can it compare idealized Christianity with less pure forms or even distorted forms of other faiths. At the same time, true dialogue must not seek to synthesize or to find agreement in the lowest common denominator. We will do well to heed Ruether's comment: "to impose one religion on everyone flattens and impoverishes the wealth of human interaction with God, much as imposing one language on everyone steals other peoples' culture, and memories" (1982,

p. 67). When we learn to listen to and respect others' experiences, our own horizons will be broadened and our world enriched.

One important key for fostering genuine interfaith dialogue is to remember that "doctrines alienate, while stories unite" (Song, 1990, p. 171). I would add that praying and singing together can also be unifying experiences since both tap into our affective, as well as our cognitive, selves. It is important to be sensitive to images that are inclusive and to avoid those that exclude as we pray and sing. I have been distressed when people unthinkingly pray "in the name of Jesus" at interfaith gatherings.

Because religion relates to experiencing and expressing the sacred, it is always embedded in a particular culture and manifests itself in community stories. So it is that the Buddha will continue to be associated with the Bo Tree, Jesus will be associated with dying on a cross and being resurrected, and Moses will continue to be understood as God's instrument in saving God's people through the Exodus (Koyama, 1988, pp. 129–130).

Because stories unite us, we might be helped to see by this story from the Buddhist scriptures:

> It is as if a man had been wounded by an arrow thickly smeared with poison, and his friends, companions, relatives, and kinsmen were to get a surgeon to heal him, and he were to say, "I will not have this arrow pulled out, until I know by what man I was wounded, whether he is of the warrior caste, or a brahmin, or the agricultural, or the lowest caste." Or if he were to say, "I will not have this arrow pulled out until I know of what name or family the man is . . . or whether he is tall or short, or of middle height . . . or whether he is black, or dark, or yellowish . . . or whether he comes from such and such a village, or town, or city . . . whether the bow with which I was wounded was a chapa or a kondanda . . . whether the bow-string was of swallow-wort, or bamboo-fibre, or sinew, or hemp . . . whether the shaft was from a wild or cultivated plant. . . ." That man would die . . . without knowing all this [quoted by Song, 1990, pp. 173–174].

The need for conceptual breakthroughs seems to be universal. It is one that all who inhabit the globe are called to meet.

There are guidelines (Cox, 1988a, pp. 11–18) that may help

Christians (for this is the only faith stance from which I am qualified to speak) as we embark on a journey toward interfaith dialogue. Those of other faiths may be able to adapt or use these guidelines, as well.

1.   Rather than moving toward abstract principles that attempt to provide a common meeting ground, focus on Jesus and speak about who Jesus is and what Jesus means to us.

2.   Avoid a stance reflecting the attitude that sincerity of belief matters more than substance; instead, concentrate on Jesus' insistence that "You will know them by their fruits. . . ." (Matt. 7:16). Remember how many surprises there were for the religious in Jesus' day and how many there are for us when we come to the gospels with new eyes and when we listen to Christians from other cultures and perspectives.

3.   Follow Jesus' example by knowing when to speak the truth in love and when to refrain from making judgments. It is clear that Jesus always began where people were, rather than where he may have wished they were or expected them to be. Seek to understand the motive as well as the act.

4.   Come to the dialogue expecting to meet God in those with whom we speak and recognizing that it is risky and that we may never be the same again; at the same time, remember that Christians have a long tradition that attests to the reality that "Christ meets us in and through the stranger." This expectation invites us to come with a spirit of openness to whatever God may have in store for us.

Many Christians struggle with questions relating to scripture asserting that Jesus is "the door" and "the way" and that persons can only come to God through the son (see especially, John 14:6). At the same time (and in the same chapter of John's gospel), Jesus states, "In my Father's house there are many dwelling places" (John 14:2). Cox suggests a helpful way of dealing with these paradoxical statements when he says: "From Jesus I have learned both that he is the Way and that in God's house there are many mansions. I do not believe these two sayings are contradictory. In fact, I have come to see that only by understanding one can we come to understand the other" (Cox, 1988a, p. 19).

As Dunne has observed, the spiritual task for our day may be "passing over" into another's way of knowing and seeing and then "coming back" with deeper and wider understanding because we see our own faith story in a different light. Passing over is not to be engaged in lightly. It cannot be for the purpose of converting others to our ways of being in faith; neither can it be done as an uninvolved and objective outsider. Rather, it is an odyssey, which starts in our homeland, leads us through the wonderland of other faith stories and communities, and takes us home again—as transformed and more compassionate persons (1972).

Interfaith dialogue invites *all* persons to join in an exploration of what it means to be human, what it means to tend the planet and universe in which we live lovingly. It beckons us to explore how we can work together to create a world where persons can work toward justice-seeking peace and gracious mercy. Together we may be able to endow others and to be endowed by them, as we share and celebrate each others' stories and traditions, our silence and our songs, our prayers and our dances, our bread (or rice or potatoes) and wine, our sorrow and our hope, our work and our play. And in this sharing, we will discover that we are journeying together toward *shalom-salem*—God's peace.

Envisioning Our Future

Adult religious education needs to provide communities of faith with *visions* and *tools* for

> Sharing stories
> Making connections within ourselves, with others in
>   our faith communities, with other faith communi-
>   ties both within and beyond our own faith tradition,
>   with *all* persons who seek to work for common
>   goals.
> Using an approach based on dialogue and media-
>   tion—both personally and institutionally,
> Rejecting arrogance and hierarchical models that create
>   the possibility of "pulling rank,"
> Accepting the dignity and right of *all* to be equal
>   partners in the dialogue,

Trading ladders for lattices in order to affirm and
empower the contributions of all,
Growing into a global identity of self and faith,
Inviting those who have been denied voice to name
their pain and claim the promise,
Showing that learning is lifelong, life-encompassing,
journeying in and toward faith,
Risking the opportunity and responsibility to share
one's own faith story, to receive the faith stories of
others, as we seek to be open to the Spirit of God,
Critically examining the lenses through which we see
and seeking to examine life from other perspectives,
Speaking in truth and love,
Keeping silent in truth and love,
Expanding horizons, sharing the particularity of our
faith, hearing the particularities of others' faiths,
bursting through boundaries,
Learning to live with and find power and beauty in
paradox as we recognize that the
    calling,
    loving,
    creating,
    judging,
    crying,
    laughing,
Mysterious One
can never be limited by our human finiteness and yet
that the Mysterious One invites *all* to share in the
work toward and joy of a just and agape-wrapped
eternity.

REFERENCES

Apps, J. W. *Improving Practice in Continuing Education: Modern Approaches for Understanding the Field and Determining Priorities.* San Francisco: Jossey-Bass, 1985.

Ashbrook, J. B. "Making Sense of Soul and Sabbath: Brain Processes and the Making of Meaning." First Annual Leroy G. Kerney Lectureship in Chaplaincy and Pastoral Care, Department of Spiritual Ministry, National Institutes of Health, Oct. 23, 1989.

Baum, G. *Religion and Alienation: A Theological Reading of Sociology.* New York: Paulist Press, 1975.

Bausch, W. J. *Storytelling: Imagination and Faith.* Mystic, Conn.: Twenty-Third Publications, 1984.

Belenky, M. F., Clinchy, B. M., Goldberger, N. R., and Tarule, J. M. *Women's Ways of Knowing: The Development of Self, Voice, and Mind.* New York: Basic Books, 1986.

Benson, P. L., and Eklin, C. H. *Effective Christian Education: A National Study of Protestant Congregations.* Summary Report on Faith, Loyalty, and Congregational Life. Minneapolis, Minn.: Search Institute, Mar. 1990.

Berger, P. L., and Luckmann, T. *The Social Construction of Reality.* New York: Anchor Books, 1967.

The Bethel Series (Bethel Series, P.O. Box 8398, Madison, Wis. 53708).

Blair, E. P. *The Illustrated Bible Handbook.* Nashville, Tenn.: Abingdon, 1987.

Bloom, B. S., and others. *Taxonomy of Educational Objectives.*
Handbook I: *Cognitive Domain.* New York: David McKay, 1956.

Blumberg, S. H., and Borowitz, E. B. "Religious Pluralism: A Jewish Perspective." In N. H. Thompson (ed.), *Religious Pluralism
and Religious Education.* Birmingham, Ala.: Religious Education Press, 1988.

Boys, M. C. "Access to Traditions and Transformation." In P.
O'Hare (ed.), *Tradition and Transformation in Religious Education.* Birmingham, Ala.: Religious Education Press, 1979.

Boys, M. C. *Educating in Faith: Maps and Visions.* New York:
Harper & Row, 1989a.

Boys, M. C. (ed.) *Education for Citizenship and Discipleship.* New
York: Pilgrim Press, 1989b.

Boys, M. C. "To Think Passionately About the World." In N. G.
Slater (ed.), *Tensions Between Citizenship and Discipleship: A
Case Study.* New York: Pilgrim Press, 1989c.

Brennan, J. G. "Alfred North Whitehead: Plato's Lost Dialogue."
In J. Epstein (ed.), *Masters: Portraits of Great Teachers.* New
York: Basic Books, 1981.

Brookfield, S. D. (ed.) *Self-Directed Learning: From Theory to Practice.* New Directions for Continuing Education, no. 25. San Francisco: Jossey-Bass, 1985.

Brookfield, S. D. *Understanding and Facilitating Adult Learning:
A Comprehensive Analysis of Principles and Effective Practices.*
San Francisco: Jossey-Bass, 1986.

Brookfield, S. D. *Developing Critical Thinkers: Challenging Adults
to Explore Alternative Ways of Thinking and Acting.* San Francisco, Jossey-Bass, 1987.

Brown, R. E. *The Anchor Bible: The Gospel According to John I–
XII.* Vol. 29. New York: Doubleday, 1966.

Brown, R. M. *Robert McAfee Brown: Creative Dislocation—The
Movement of Grace.* Nashville, Tenn.: Abingdon, 1980.

Brown, R. M. *Unexpected News: Reading the Bible with Third
World Eyes.* Philadelphia: Westminster Press, 1984.

Brown, R. M. "What Can North Americans Learn from Minjung
Theology?" In J. Y. Lee (ed.), *An Emerging Theology in World
Perspective: Commentary on Korean Minjung Theology.* Mystic,
Conn.: Twenty-Third Publications, 1988.

Browning, R. L. *The Pastor as Religious Educator.* Birmingham, Ala.: Religious Education Press, 1989.

Browning, R. L., and Reed, R. A. *The Sacraments in Religious Education and Liturgy.* Birmingham, Ala.: Religious Education Press, 1985.

Brueggemann, W. *The Creative Word: Canon as a Model for Biblical Education.* Philadelphia: Fortress, 1982.

Brueggemann, W. "The Legitimacy of a Sectarian Hermeneutic: 2 Kings 18–19." In M. C. Boys (ed.), *Education for Citizenship and Discipleship.* New York: Pilgrim Press, 1989.

Brueggemann, W., Parks, S., and Groome, T. H. *To Act Justly, Love Tenderly, Walk Humbly: An Agenda for Ministers.* New York: Paulist Press, 1986.

Butkus, R. A. "Christian Education for Peace and Social Justice: Perspectives from the Thought of John Dewey and Paulo Freire." In P. O'Hare (ed.), *Education for Peace and Justice.* Harper & Row, 1983.

Cardenal, E. *The Gospel in Solentiname.* 4 vols. Maryknoll, N.Y.: Orbis, 1976–1982.

Coe, G. A. *A Social Theory of Religious Education.* New York: Scribner's, 1917.

Coles, R. *The Call of Stories: Teaching and the Moral Imagination.* Boston: Houghton Mifflin, 1989.

Cox, H. *Just As I Am.* Nashville, Tenn.: Abingdon, 1983.

Cox, H. *Many Mansions: A Christian's Encounter with Other Faiths.* Boston: Beacon Press, 1988a.

Cox, H. "The Religion of Ordinary People: Toward a North American Minjung Theology." In J. Y. Lee (ed.), *An Emerging Theology in World Perspective: Commentary on Korean Minjung Theology.* Mystic, Conn.: Twenty-Third Publications, 1988b.

Cross, K. P. *Adults as Learners: Increasing Participation and Facilitating Learning.* San Francisco: Jossey-Bass, 1981.

Daloz, L. A. *Effective Teaching and Mentoring: Realizing the Transformational Power of Adult Learning Experiences.* San Francisco: Jossey-Bass, 1986.

Disciple (Disciple Bible Study, Rm. 248, P.O. Box 801, Nashville, Tenn. 37202).

Duck, R. C., and Bausch, M. G. (eds.). *Everflowing Streams: Songs for Worship.* New York: Pilgrim Press, 1981.

Dunne, J. S. *The Way of All the Earth: Experiments in Truth and Religion.* South Bend, Ind.: University of Notre Dame Press, 1972.

Dykstra, C. "My Teacher, We Made Bread . . . ." *The Christian Century,* Oct. 1, 1980, p. 901.

Dykstra, C. *Vision and Character: A Christian Educator's Alternative to Kohlberg.* New York: Paulist Press, 1981.

Elias, J. L. *The Foundations and Practice of Adult Religious Education.* 2nd ed. Malabar, Fla.: Krieger, 1986.

Eliot, T. S. *The Elder Statesman.* New York: Farrar, Straus & Giroux, 1959.

Endo, S. *Silence.* (W. Johnston, trans.). Tokyo: Sophia University, 1969.

Erikson, E. H. *Identity and the Life Cycle.* New York: Norton, 1980.

Evans, A. F., Evans, R. A., and Kennedy, W. B. *Pedagogies for the Non-Poor.* Maryknoll, N.Y.: Orbis, 1987.

Felder, C. H. *Troubling Biblical Waters: Race, Class, and Family.* Maryknoll, N.Y.: Orbis, 1989.

Fishbane, M. *Text and Texture: Close Readings of Selected Biblical Texts.* New York: Schocken Books, 1979.

Fishbane, M. *Biblical Interpretation in Ancient Israel.* Oxford, England: Clarendon Press, 1985.

Foltz, N. T. (ed.). *Handbook of Adult Religious Education.* Birmingham, Ala.: Religious Education Press, 1986.

Forester, J. *Planning in the Face of Power.* Berkeley: University of California Press, 1989.

Foster, C. R. "The Faith Community As a Guiding Image in Christian Education." In J. L. Seymour and D. E. Miller (eds.), *Contemporary Approaches to Christian Education.* Nashville, Tenn.: Abingdon, 1982.

Foster, C. R. *The Ministry of the Volunteer Teacher.* Nashville, Tenn.: Abingdon, 1986.

Fowler, J. W. *Stages of Faith: The Psychology of Human Development and the Quest for Meaning.* New York: Harper & Row, 1981.

Fowler, J. W. "Stages of Faith and Adults' Life Cycles." In K. Stokes (ed.), *Faith Development in the Adult Life Cycle*. New York: W. H. Sadlier, 1982.

Fowler, J. W. *Becoming Adult, Becoming Christian*. New York: Harper & Row, 1984.

Fox, M. *Original Blessing*. Santa Fe, N.M.: Bear, 1983.

Fox, M. *The Cosmic Christ: The Healing of Mother Earth and the Birth of a Global Renaissance*. New York: Harper & Row, 1988.

Freire, P. *Pedagogy of the Oppressed*. New York: Seabury Press, 1970.

Galdamez, P. *Faith of a People*. Maryknoll, N.Y.: Orbis, 1986.

Gillespie, V. B. *The Experience of Faith*. Birmingham, Ala.: Religious Education Press, 1988.

Gilligan, C. *In a Different Voice: Psychological Theory and Women's Development*. Cambridge, Mass.: Harvard University Press, 1977.

Glass, J. C., Jr. *Growing Through Adulthood: Can the Church Help?* Nashville, Tenn.: Discipleship Resources, 1979.

Gould, S. J. *Wonderful Life: The Burgess Shale and the Nature of History*. New York: Norton, 1989.

Grabowski, S. and Mason, W. D. (eds.). *Learning for Aging*. Washington, D.C.: Adult Education Association of the U.S.A., 1976.

Grierson, D. *Transforming a People of God*. Melbourne: Joint Board of Christian Education of Australia and New Zealand, 1984.

Groome, T. H. *Christian Religious Education*. New York: Harper & Row, 1980.

Gutierrez, G. *We Drink from Our Own Wells: The Spiritual Journey of a People*. Maryknoll, N.Y.: Orbis, 1984.

Guzie, T. *The Book of Sacramental Basics*. New York: Paulist Press, 1981.

Harris, M. "Word, Sacrament, Prophecy." In P. O'Hare (ed.), *Tradition and Transformation in Religious Education*. Birmingham, Ala.: Religious Education Press, 1979.

Harris, M. *Teaching and Religious Imagination*. New York: Harper & Row, 1987.

Harris, M. *Women and Teaching*. New York: Paulist Press, 1988.

Harris, M. *Dance of the Spirit: The Seven Steps of Women's Spirituality*. New York: Bantam Books, 1989a.

Harris, M. *Fashion Me A People*. Louisville, Ky.: John Knox Press, 1989b.

Hawkes, M., and Hamill, P. *Sing to God*. New York: United Church Press, 1984, p. 192.

Heilbrun, C. G. *Writing a Woman's Life*. New York: Norton, 1988.

Herzberger, M. *The Waltz of the Shadows*. New York: Philosophical Library, 1983.

Heschel, A. J. *The Sabbath: Its Meaning for Modern Man*. New York: Farrar, Straus & Giroux, 1951.

Heschel, A. J. *The Prophets*. 2 vols. New York: Harper & Row, Torchbooks, 1962.

Heschel, A. J. *A Passion for Truth*. New York: Farrar, Straus & Giroux, 1973.

Hickman, H. L., Saliers, D. E., Stookey, L. H., and White, J. F. *Handbook of the Christian Year*. Nashville, Tenn.: Abingdon, 1986.

Holy Bible. New Revised Standard Version. Nashville, Tenn.: Thomas Nelson Publishers, 1989.

Isaacs, H. *Scratches on Our Minds: American Views of China and India*. New York: John Day, 1958. Reprint. White Plains, N.Y.: M. E. Sharpe, 1980.

Jenkins, D. E. *Still Living with Questions*. London: SCM Press, 1990.

Johnson, S. "Education in the Images of God." In J. L. Seymour and D. E. Miller (eds.), *Theological Approaches to Christian Education*. Nashville, Tenn.: Abingdon, 1990.

Jones, A. W. *Soul Making: The Desert Way of Spirituality*. New York: Harper & Row, 1985.

Jones, W. P. *Theological Worlds: Understanding the Alternative Rhythms of Christian Belief*. Nashville, Tenn.: Abingdon, 1989.

Joyce, B., and Weil, M. *Models of Teaching*. 3rd ed. Englewood Cliffs, N.J.: Prentice-Hall, 1986.

Jung, C. G. *Modern Man in Search of a Soul*. San Diego, Calif.: Harcourt Brace Jovanovich, 1933.

Kaufman, G. D. *The Theological Imagination: Constructing the Concept of God*. Philadelphia: Westminster Press, 1981.

Keen, S. *The Passionate Life: Stages of Loving*. New York: Harper & Row, 1983.

Kegan, R. *The Evolving Self: Problems and Process in Human Development.* Cambridge, Mass.: Harvard University Press, 1982.

Kennedy, W. B. "Ideology and Education: A Fresh Approach for Religious Education." *Religious Education,* 1985, *80* (3), 331–344.

Kerygma (Kerygma Program, 300 Mt. Lebanon Blvd., Suite 205, Pittsburgh, Penn. 15234).

Khouj, A. M. "Education in Islam." In N. H. Thompson (ed.), *Religious Pluralism and Religious Education.* Birmingham, Ala.: Religious Education Press, 1988.

Kidd, J. R. *How Adults Learn.* Rev. ed. Chicago: Follett, 1973.

Knowles, M. S. *Self-Directed Learning: A Guide for Learners and Teachers.* New York: Cambridge Book Company, 1975.

Knowles, M. S. *The Modern Practice of Adult Education.* Rev. ed. New York: Cambridge Book Company, 1980.

Knowles, M. S. *The Adult Learner: A Neglected Species.* 3rd ed. Houston, Tex.: Gulf, 1984.

Knowles, M. S. *The Making of an Adult Educator: An Autobiographical Journey.* San Francisco: Jossey-Bass, 1989.

Knox, A. B. *Adult Development and Learning: A Handbook on Individual Growth and Competence in the Adult Years.* San Francisco: Jossey-Bass, 1977.

Knox, A. B. *Helping Adults Learn: A Guide to Planning, Implementating, and Conducting Programs.* San Francisco: Jossey-Bass, 1986.

Koyama, K. " 'Building the House by Righteousness': The Ecumenical Horizons of Minjung Theology." In J. Y. Lee (ed.), *An Emerging Theology in World Perspective: Commentary on Korean Minjung Theology.* Mystic, Conn.: Twenty-Third Publications, 1988.

Krathwohl, D. R., Bloom, B., and Masia, B. *Taxonomy of Educational Objectives.* Handbook 2: *Affective Domain.* New York: David McKay, 1964.

Küng, H. *On Being a Christian.* New York: Doubleday, 1976.

Lang, M. A. *Acquiring Our Image of God: Emotional Basis for Religious Education.* New York: Paulist Press, 1983.

Lebacqz, K. "Pain and Pedagogy: A Modest Proposal." In M. C.

Boys (ed.), *Education for Citizenship and Discipleship*. New York: Pilgrim Press, 1989.

Lee, J. M. *The Shape of Religious Instruction: A Social Science Approach*. Birmingham, Ala.: Religious Education Press, 1971.

Lee, J. M. *The Flow of Religious Instruction: A Social Science Approach*. Birmingham, Ala.: Religious Education Press, 1973.

Lee, J. M. (ed.). *The Religious Education We Need: Toward the Renewal of Christian Education*. Birmingham, Ala.: Religious Education Press, 1977.

Lee, J. M. *The Content of Religious Instruction*. Birmingham, Ala.: Religious Education Press, 1985.

Lee, J. Y. (ed.). *An Emerging Theology in World Perspective: Commentary on Korean Minjung Theology*. Mystic, Conn.: Twenty-Third Publications, 1988.

LeFevre, C., and LeFevre, P. (eds.). *Aging and the Human Spirit*. Chicago: Exploration Press, 1981.

Levenson, J. D. *Siani and Zion: An Entry into the Jewish Bible*. Minneapolis, Minn.: Winston Press, 1985.

Levinson, D. J. *The Seasons of a Man's Life*. New York: Knopf, 1978.

Lewis, C. S. *The Last Battle*. New York: Collier Books, 1956.

Little, S. "Religious Instruction." In J. L. Seymour and D. E. Miller (eds.), *Contemporary Approaches to Christian Education*. Nashville, Tenn.: Abingdon, 1982.

Little, S. *To Set One's Heart: Belief and Teaching in the Church*. Atlanta, Ga.: John Knox Press, 1983.

Loder, J. E. *The Transforming Moment*. 2nd ed. Colorado Springs, Colo.: Helmers & Howard, 1989.

Maas, R. *Church Bible-Study Handbook*. Nashville, Tenn.: Abingdon, 1982.

McClusky, H. Y. "Education for Aging: The Scope of the Field and Perspectives for the Future." In S. Grabowski and W. D. Mason (eds.), *Learning for Aging*. Washington, D.C.: Adult Education Association of the U.S.A., 1976.

McFague, S. *Metaphorical Theology: Models of God in Religious Language*. Philadelphia: Fortress, 1982.

McFague, S. *Models of God: Theology for an Ecological, Nuclear Age*. Philadelphia: Fortress, 1987.

Maitland, D. J. *Looking Both Ways: A Theology for Mid-Life.* Atlanta, Ga.: John Knox Press, 1985.

Maitland, D. J. *Aging as Counterculture: A Vocation for the Later Years.* New York: Pilgrim Press, 1991.

Marthaler, B. L. "Socialization as a Model for Catechetics." In P. O'Hare (ed.), *Foundations of Religious Education.* New York: Paulist Press, 1978.

Martin, J. R. *Reclaiming a Conversation: The Ideal of the Educated Woman.* New Haven, Conn.: Yale University Press, 1985.

Maslow, A. H. *Motivation and Personality.* 2nd ed. New York: Harper & Row, 1970.

Matsuoka, F. "The Church in a Racial-Minority Situation." In J. L. Seymour and D. E. Miller (eds.), *Theological Approaches to Christian Education.* Nashville, Tenn.: Abingdon, 1990.

May, M. "Tradition and Education." In J. L. Seymour and D. E. Miller (eds.), *Theological Approaches to Christian Education.* Nashville, Tenn.: Abingdon, 1990.

Merriam, S. B., and Ferro, T. R. "Working with Young Adults." In N. T. Foltz (ed.), *Handbook of Adult Religious Education.* Birmingham, Ala.: Religious Education Press, 1986.

Merritt, D. "Ecumenical Learning in a Global Perspective." In J. L. Seymour and D. E. Miller (eds.), *Theological Approaches to Christian Education.* Nashville, Tenn.: Abingdon, 1990.

Mezirow, J. "A Critical Theory of Adult Learning and Education." In S. D. Brookfield (ed.), *Self-Directed Learning: From Theory to Practice.* New Directions for Continuing Education, no. 25. San Francisco: Jossey-Bass, 1985.

Miller, D. E. "The Developmental Approach to Christian Education." In J. L. Seymour and D. E. Miller (eds.), *Contemporary Approaches to Christian Education.* Nashville, Tenn.: Abingdon, 1982.

Miller, D. E. *Story and Context: An Introduction to Christian Education.* Nashville, Tenn.: Abingdon, 1987.

Miller, D. E., Snyder, G. F., and Neff, R. W. *Using Biblical Simulations.* Vols. 1 and 2. Valley Forge, Penn.: Judson Press, 1971, 1975.

Moltmann, J. *Creating a Just Future.* London: SCM Press, 1989.

Monette, M. L. "Educational Planning: Responding Responsibly."

In Parent, N. (ed.), *Christian Adulthood: A Catechetical Resource.* Washington, D.C.: United States Catholic Conference, 1982.

Monette, M. L. "Justice, Peace, and the Pedagogy of Grass Roots Christian Community." In P. O'Hare (ed.), *Education for Peace and Justice.* New York: Harper & Row, 1983.

Moore, A. J. "Liberation and the Future of Christian Education." In J. L. Seymour and D. E. Miller (eds.), *Contemporary Approaches to Christian Education.* Nashville, Tenn.: Abingdon, 1982.

Moore, M. E. *Education for Continuity and Change: A New Model for Christian Religious Education.* Nashville, Tenn.: Abingdon, 1983.

Moore, M. E. "Feminist Theology and Education." In J. L. Seymour and D. E. Miller (eds.), *Theological Approaches to Christian Education.* Nashville, Tenn.: Abingdon, 1990.

Moran, G. *Religious Education Development: Images for the Future.* Minneapolis, Minn.: Winston Press, 1983.

Moran, G. *Religious Education as a Second Language.* Birmingham, Ala.: Religious Education Press, 1989.

Morgan, P. M. *Story Weaving: Using Stories to Transform Your Congregation.* St. Louis, Mo.: CBP Press, 1986.

Morrison, M. C. *Approaching the Gospels Together.* Wallingford, Penn.: Pendle Hill, 1986.

Moseley, R. "Education and Human Development in the Likeness of Christ." In J. L. Seymour and D. E. Miller (eds.), *Theological Approaches to Christian Education.* Nashville, Tenn.: Abingdon, 1990.

Mulholland, M. R., Jr. *Shaped by the Word: The Power of the Scripture in Spiritual Formation.* Nashville, Tenn.: The Upper Room, 1985.

Murray, D. *Teaching the Bible to Adults and Youth.* Nashville, Tenn.: Abingdon, 1987.

Nelson, E. *How Faith Matures.* Louisville, Ky.: Westminster-John Knox Press, 1989.

Nelson, E. *Where Faith Begins.* Atlanta, Ga.: John Knox Press, 1976.

Nelson-Pallmeyer, J. *War Against the Poor: Low-Intensity Conflict and Christian Faith.* Maryknoll, N.Y.: Orbis, 1989.

Neugarten, B. L. *Middle Age and Aging.* Chicago: University of Chicago Press, 1968.

Niebuhr, R. "A View from the Pew." *Christian Century*, 1984, *101* (40), 1197.

Nouwen, H. *A Cry for Mercy: Prayers from the Genesee.* Garden City, N.Y.: Image Books, 1983.

Nouwen, H. *Reaching Out: The Three Movements of the Spiritual Life.* Garden City, N.Y.: Image Books, 1986.

Oh, Y. B., and Park, S. Y. "Buddhist Education and Religious Pluralism." In N. H. Thompson (ed.), *Religious Pluralism and Religious Education.* Birmingham, Ala.: Religious Education Press, 1988.

O'Hare, P. (ed.). *Foundations of Religious Education.* New York: Paulist Press, 1978.

O'Hare, P. *Tradition and Transformation in Religious Education.* Birmingham, Ala.: Religious Education Press, 1979.

Osmer, R. R. *A Teachable Spirit: Recovering the Teaching Office in the Church.* Louisville, Ky.: Westminster-John Knox Press, 1990.

Palmer, P. J. *In the Belly of a Paradox: A Celebration of Contradictions in the Thought of Thomas Merton.* Pamplet 224. Wallingford, Penn.: Pendle Hill, 1979.

Palmer, P. J. *The Company of Strangers: Christians and the Renewal of America's Public Life.* New York: Crossroad, 1981.

Palmer, P. J. *To Know as We Are Known: A Spirituality of Education.* New York: Harper & Row, 1983.

Parks, S. *The Critical Years.* New York: Harper & Row, 1986.

Perry, W. G. *Forms of Intellectual and Ethical Development in the College Years: A Scheme.* New York: Holt, Rinehart & Winston, 1968.

Peterson, D. A. *Facilitating Education for Older Learners.* San Francisco: Jossey-Bass, 1983.

Pobee, J. S., and von Wartenberg-Potter, B. *New Eyes for Reading.* Oak Park, Ill.: Meyer-Stone, 1986.

Postman, N., and Weingartner, C. *Teaching as a Subversive Activity.* New York: Dell, 1969.

Raines, R. *Living the Questions.* Waco, Tex.: Word Books, 1975.

Raines, R. *The Gift of Tomorrow.* Nashville, Tenn.: Abingdon, 1984.

Richardson, E. A. *Strangers in This Land: Pluralism and the Response to Diversity in the United States.* New York: Pilgrim Press, 1988.

Rilke, R. M. *Letters to a Young Poet.* New York: Norton, 1934.

Rogers, C. *Freedom to Learn.* Westerville, Ohio: Merrill, 1969.

Ruether, R. R. *Disputed Questions: On Being a Christian.* Nashville, Tenn.: Abingdon, 1982.

Ruether, R. R. *Sexism and God-Talk.* Boston: Beacon Press, 1983.

Russell, L. M. "Handing on Traditions and Changing the World." In P. O'Hare (ed.), *Tradition and Transformation in Religious Education.* Birmingham, Ala.: Religious Education Press, 1979.

Russell, L. M. *Household of Freedom.* Philadelphia: Westminster Press, 1987.

Russell, L. M. "Minjung Theology in Women's Perspective." In J. Y. Lee (ed.), *An Emerging Theology in World Perspective: Commentary on Korean Minjung Theology.* Mystic, Conn.: Twenty-Third Publications, 1988.

Sawicki, M. *The Gospel in History: Portrait of a Teaching Church, The Origins of Christian Education.* New York: Paulist Press, 1988.

Sawicki, M. "Tradition and Sacramental Education." In J. L. Seymour and D. E. Miller (eds.), *Theological Approaches to Christian Education.* Nashville, Tenn.: Abingdon, 1990.

Schipani, D. S. *Conscientization and Creativity: Paulo Freire and Christian Education.* Lanham, Md.: University Press of America, 1984.

Seymour, J. L., and Miller, D. E. (eds.). *Contemporary Approaches to Christian Education.* Nashville, Tenn.: Abingdon, 1982.

Seymour, J. L., and Miller, D. E. (eds.). *Theological Approaches to Christian Education.* Nashville, Tenn.: Abingdon, 1990.

Seymour, J. L., O'Gorman, R. T., and Foster, C. R. *Church in the Education of the Public.* Nashville, Tenn.: Abingdon, 1984.

Slater, N. G. (ed.). *Tensions Between Citizenship and Discipleship: A Case Study.* New York: Pilgrim Press, 1989.

Smith, H. *The Religions of Man.* New York: Harper & Row, 1958.

Snyder, R. "In the Aging Years: Spirit." In C. LeFevre and P. LeFevre (eds.), *Aging and the Human Spirit.* Chicago: Exploration Press, 1981.

Song, C. S. *Tell Us Our Names: Story Theology from an Asian Perspective.* Maryknoll, N.Y.: Orbis, 1987.

Song, C. S. "Christian Education in a World of Religious Pluralism." In J. L. Seymour and D. E. Miller (eds.), *Theological Approaches to Christian Education.* Nashville, Tenn.: Abingdon, 1990.

Sparkman, G. T. "The Pastor as Leader of an Educational Team." In Robert L. Browning (ed.), *The Pastor as Religious Educator.* Birmingham, Ala.: Religious Education Press, 1989.

Stegner, R. *Narrative Theology in Early Jewish Christianity.* Louisville, Ky.: Westminster-John Knox Press, 1989.

Stein, J. *Fiddler on the Roof.* New York: Crown, 1964.

Sternberg, R. J. *Metaphors of Mind: Conceptions of the Nature of Intelligence.* Cambridge, England: Cambridge University Press, 1990.

Takenaka, M. *God Is Rice: Asian Culture and Christian Faith.* Geneva, Switzerland: World Council of Churches, 1986.

Tamez, E. *Bible of the Oppressed.* Maryknoll, N.Y.: Orbis, 1982.

Tathagatananda, S. "Hinduism and How It Is Transmitted." In N. H. Thompson (ed.), *Religious Pluralism and Religious Education.* Birmingham, Ala.: Religious Education Press, 1988.

Theobald, R. *The Rapids of Change: Social Entrepreneurship in Turbulent Times.* Indianapolis, Ind.: Knowledge Systems, 1987.

Thompson, N. H. *Religious Pluralism and Religious Education.* Birmingham, Ala.: Religious Education Press, 1988.

Thurian, M., and Wainwright, G. (eds.). *Baptism and Eucharist: Ecumenical Convergence in Celebration.* Geneva, Switzerland: WCC Publications, 1983.

To Teach As Jesus Did. Pastoral Message on Catholic Education by the National Conference of Catholic Bishops. Pastoral letter no. 44. Washington, D.C.: United States Catholic Conference, 1973.

Tobin, M. L. *Hope Is an Open Door.* Nashville, Tenn.: Abingdon, 1981.

Toffler, A. *The Third Wave.* New York: Morrow, 1980.

Tough, A. *The Adult's Learning Projects: A Fresh Approach to Theory and Practice in Adult Learning.* 2nd ed. Toronto: Ontario Institute for Studies in Education, 1979.

Vogel, L. J. "How Older Adults Perceive and Legitimize Their Adult Education Participation in Schools and Churches." Unpublished Ph.D. dissertation, University of Iowa, May 1981.

Vogel, L. J. *The Religious Education of Older Adults.* Birmingham, Ala.: Religious Education Press, 1984.

Walker, A. *The Color Purple.* San Diego, Calif.: Harcourt Brace Jovanovich, 1982.

Wallis, J. *Revive Us Again: A Sojourner's Story.* Nashville, Tenn.: Abingdon, 1983.

Wartenberg-Potter, B. von. *We Will Not Hang Our Harps on the Willows.* Oak Park, Ill.: Meyer-Stone, 1988.

Waters, F. *The Man Who Killed the Deer: A Novel of Pueblo Indian Life.* Beverly Hills, Calif.: Sage, 1942.

Weber, H. R. *Experiments with Bible Study.* Geneva, Switzerland: World Council of Churches, 1981.

Weems, R. *Just a Sister Away.* San Diego, Calif.: LuraMedia, 1988.

Westerhoff, J. H., III. *A Pilgrim People: Learning Through the Church Year.* New York: Harper & Row, 1984.

Westerhoff, J. H., III. *Living the Faith Community: The Church That Makes a Difference.* Minneapolis, Minn.: Winston Press, 1985.

White, J. F. *Sacraments as God's Self-Giving.* Nashville, Tenn.: Abingdon, 1983.

Whitehead, A. N. *The Aims of Education and Other Essays.* New York: Macmillan, 1929.

Whitehead, J. D., and Whitehead, E. E. *Method in Ministry: Theological Reflection and Christian Ministry.* New York: Seabury Press, 1980.

Wilkes, P. "The Changing and Often Troubled World of American Seminaries." *The Atlantic,* Dec. 1990.

Williams, M. E. "Story as Oral Experience." *Explor,* 1979, 5 (2) 2–11.

Wink, W. *The Bible in Human Transformation: Toward a New Paradigm for Biblical Study.* Philadelphia: Fortress, 1973.

Wink, W. *Transforming Bible Study: A Leader's Guide.* Nashville, Tenn.: Abingdon, 1980.

Wlodkowski, R. J. *Enhancing Adult Motivation to Learn: A Guide to Improving Instruction and Increasing Learner Achievement.* San Francisco: Jossey-Bass, 1985.

Wren, B. *Education for Justice: Pedagogical Principles.* Maryknoll, N.Y.: Orbis, 1977.

INDEX

107065

Printed in the United States
1335200003B/166